FAITH ON FILM

To Ashleigh,

Enjoy

'First, it's a great read. It will either encourage you to go see the films Andy has reviewed or help you to realise that you don't need to! Second, it's a thought-provoking read. It may well take you into areas of exploration that you've not encountered before, either about films or about faith. Andy speaks and writes with insider knowledge and integrity in equal measure.

'Finally, it's not just an interesting book to read and learn from; it's also a resource to be used as a discussion-starter and conversation-continuer! It's a great example of what every self-respecting 'likely to make me think' book should have: namely, some questions to help you explore further, engage with others, and journey onwards in life, having been expanded in mind and enriched in soul.'

Stuart Pascall, former tutor and head of evangelism at Moorlands College

'Andy takes a light-hearted look at the films he's passionate about and gives us fun little insights along the way. He perfectly articulates what it's like to be a fully paid-up member of the 'churches' of Christianity and film criticism – two cultures that don't always sit well with each other. This book has also given me plenty of inspiration for new films to cover!'

Giles Gough, host, God in Film podcast

'An intelligent, pragmatic and perceptive evaluation of the genre of film and cinema. Should be on the required reading list of all who endeavour to communicate the gospel in a relevant way to today's generation."

Doug Barnett, pastor, evangelist and former head of evangelism at Moorlands College

'Andy Godfrey is an unashamed movie buff! His enthusiasm for all things film-related comes bursting through these pages. And so does his love for Christ and the gospel. Drawing on his vast knowledge, he passionately navigates us through "the good, the bad and the ugly" of the film world. For those of us (surely all) seeking a way to connect with people who have little or no church/Christian contact, this is a most helpful resource to have.'

Mike Mellor, evangelist, author and member of the Outreach UK Council

'For a number of years it's been a joy having Andy as Hope FM's resident film reviewer. Not many Christians have such an expansive knowledge of movies, both good and bad. He isn't scared to watch a very broad range of films to help our audience find the more family-friendly ones they will love. There are some films mentioned in this book that I know I wouldn't want to watch, but I'm glad Andy has seen them. He gives genuine insight and can speak into a culture that shouldn't be ignored. This book will not only help you enjoy films, but also see how you can use them to talk more about the goodness of God.'

Gordon T, Hope FM

'Andy's passion for Jesus and movies shines through in his musings. A wide array of intelligent and insightful reviews makes for an entertaining and informative read.'

Gordon Curley, Counties evangelist

'The good reverend takes us on an entertaining gallop through his favourite genres. A fun read – even for a heathen like me.'

Bob Mann, BBC Radio Solent

'Grab yourself a front-row seat and be entertained and enlightened by Andy Godfrey's film-fest of a book. Some may be "shaken", others may be "stirred", but it will definitely change the way we all watch movies!'

Sue Rinaldi, musician, speaker and writer

'I have known Andy Godfrey for many years and can vouch for his integrity. His book *Faith on Film* is well written and researched and easy to read, even if you are not a film boffin as he is. His insight and interpretation of films is masterly, and his ability to extract Christian concepts and statements is valuable for those looking for illustrations for their sermons. I am sure you will enjoy this book.'

Victor Jack, evangelist

'An insightful exploration connecting Andy's passion to the Passion. Andy Godfrey discusses in his typical down-to-earth tone what the world of cinema in all it's genres means to him, and how it has allowed him to come closer to God in all his full and glorious technicolor.'

Scott Forbes, Forbes TV and Film Review

'This book is a gem and a must for any film buff, and in particular any Christian who's interested in connecting with today's world and culture. I enjoyed Andy's light-hearted, speedy writing style, his detailed film knowledge and his willingness to invite you to disagree with his pick of the best of cinema. This is a great read and I thoroughly recommend it.'

Colin Johnson, evangelist with Counties Evangelism and Outreach UK

FAITH
ON
FILM

Confessions of a Christian Film Critic

ANDY GODFREY

scm

Copyright © Andy Godfrey 2024

First published in 2024 by SCM (Son Christian Media Ltd)

The right of Andy Godfrey to be identified as the author of this work has been asserted by him in accordance with the Copyright, Designs and Patents Act 1988. All rights reserved.

No part of this publication may be reproduced, stored in a retrieval system, or transmitted in any other form or by any means, electronic, mechanical, photocopying, recording or otherwise, without the prior permission of the publisher, except in the case of brief quotations embodied in critical articles or reviews.

Unless otherwise stated, Scripture quotations are from the Holy Bible, New International Version® Anglicized, NIV® Copyright © 1979, 1984, 2011 by Biblica, Inc.® Used by permission. All rights reserved worldwide.

British Library Cataloguing in Publication Data. A catalogue record for this book is available from the British Library.

ISBN: 9798326156716

Cover design © Esther Kotecha

To you, Dad, for allowing me to stay up late to watch classic science-fiction films with you, and for all those cinema trips together. You taught me how to be a preacher and introduced me to a wonderful world of entertainment. Rest in peace.

And to you, Amy. You are a wonderful daughter and an excellent film critic in your own right. Thank you for providing the inspiration for this book. I owe you a debt of gratitude.

Contents

Foreword by Steve Legg...13
Introduction: 'Why is it in that strange colour?'...........15
1 Why should the devil have all the good movies?.......19
   Intermission 1..27
2 Science-fiction double feature................................29
   Intermission 2..35
3 Do you hear the people sing?.................................37
   Intermission 3..43
4 The name's Godfrey... Andy Godfrey......................47
   Intermission 4..53
5 I'm dreaming of a movie-filled Christmas...............55
   Intermission 5..61
6 Let there be lights, camera, action! (A history of the Bible on film)..63
   Intermission 6..67
7 Making it up as we go along...................................69
   Intermission 7..75
8 His name was Alfred Hitchcock..............................77
   Intermission 8..81
9 Wishing upon a star..83
   Intermission 9..89
10 But how did it all begin?.......................................91

Intermission 10	97
11 Woya woya way, woo woo wa!	99
Intermission 11	105
12 Burning bridges	109
Intermission 12	115
100 of the best	117
Conclusion	123
Epilogue: More favourite reviews	125
Appendix: A guide to movie nights at your church	143
Acknowledgements	151

Foreword

You may be thinking, *A Christian film critic? Whatever next? A vegan butcher?* But as I delved deeper, I soon discovered that this account differs from your average movie review book.

In *Faith on Film: Confessions of a Christian Film Critic*, we are invited into a unique perspective on the world of cinema; one that seamlessly blends faith with film critique. As I delved into Andy Godfrey's insightful musings, I was struck by the depth of his analysis and the sincerity of his reflections.

Andy offers a refreshing perspective on an industry often criticised for its portrayal of morality and spirituality. With a keen eye for detail and a profound understanding of both cinema and faith, he navigates the celluloid landscape from an unapologetically Christian perspective. It's as if Barry Norman and Mark Kermode had a cinematic lovechild, armed with a big black Bible and a bucket of popcorn.

You'll soon discover that Andy's insights are as refreshing as a Sunday morning lie-in and as entertaining as a matinee double feature. He brings a wealth of knowledge and experience to the table. But what sets his work apart is his unwavering commitment to exploring the intersection of faith and film.

Through his careful critiques and thought-provoking commentary, Andy invites readers to reconsider their views on cinema and spirituality. Whether a devout believer, a film fanatic or a casual moviegoer, this book offers valuable insights that will leave a lasting impact.

So, as you embark on this journey through the lens of a Christian film critic, I encourage you to open your mind and heart to the possibilities that await. Andy offers more than just movie reviews; he provides a window into the soul of cinema itself.

Steve Legg
Editor, *Sorted* **magazine**

Introduction
'Why is it in that strange colour?'

Realising she wasn't in Kansas any more was the moment everything changed – and not just for Dorothy Gale. This was the moment everything changed for me as well. It was a cold Boxing Day in the late 1960s, and my parents had taken me and my brother to see a reissue of *The Wizard of Oz* (1939) at the Salisbury Odeon. It was my first trip to the cinema.

Initially disappointed by the film's bleak sepia tone, I remember asking Dad, 'Why is it in that strange colour?'

'Wait and see,' he whispered back.

Then it happened.

Having survived the tornado, the farmhouse crash-landed, Dorothy opened the door, and we were, in line with Bruce 'the Boss' Springsteen's song title, 'Blinded by the Light'. The full Technicolor world of Oz burst in upon us.

What a moment that was – life-changing to be honest. Suddenly it all made sense. This was fantastic. This was incredible. I was somewhere else. Somewhere my asthma and my problems at school really didn't matter at all. Somewhere I could get lost and have fun. Somewhere exciting and different. Somewhere I could have a thrilling adventure. I discovered, at that very moment, the power and joy of cinema. This was it!

So now, fifty years later, I am a film fan, a movie buff and a habitual cinemagoer. I have become a collector of all things film-related, and have a collection of nearly 3,000 movies in my home. Books on cinema fill my shelves, and my home is adorned with wall-to-wall movie posters. In addition, I have become an obsessive collector of movie soundtracks – 500 plus and counting, including many on vinyl.

In a classic case of a dream coming true, I get to write regular film reviews for Christian media outlets: *Sorted* (the UK's leading Christian magazine for men) and Konnect Radio. I've even become friends with the nation's leading film critic, Mark Kermode. I get to attend press screenings and help run a Facebook page where 6,000-plus people spend their time talking about movies.

How on earth has all this happened? If I'm honest I'm not sure… but I wouldn't change a thing.

Going to the cinema has become my favourite thing to do when heading out. Why? Because I'm going back to Oz, and I can't wait to get there. Anything can happen! I can be transported to any place at any time. I can meet characters from any period of history – even the future. I can be left in awe and wonder at specular sights; I can be informed, educated – even changed. I can be made to laugh, cry and – at times – scream! I can be taken out of my world and placed somewhere else, where nothing seems to matter, at least for a few hours.

But there's a *but*… a BIG *but*. And it's this *but* that formed the basis of my book…

A word about the 'intermissions' in this book

The intermissions feature reviews of a wide variety of films I have had published over the years in *Sorted* magazine. I was able to get to press screenings and even some premieres. Always exciting!

It may well be that some are films you have seen yourself and either liked or disliked. Please feel free to disagree with my reviews. That's part of the fun of film criticism after all.

You can follow me on Twitter @andymgodfrey1.

1
Why should the devil have all the good movies?

Let's dive straight in at the deep end and start with that *but* I mentioned in the Introduction. The *but* is simply this: I am a Christian. I am a dedicated, committed follower of Jesus Christ. So much so that, following three years of training at theological college back in the 1980s, I have spent most of the last forty years in full-time Christian work.

I believe in Jesus. I believe that he died on the cross to pay the price for the crimes of the world – including mine. I believe he literally and physically rose from the dead, and is alive today. I believe that one day he is coming back. I believe that it is only by trusting in him that a person ends up in heaven. I believe in the Bible.

That's me, and that's my position. I work for Outreach UK and write for Christian men's magazine *Sorted* and preach in churches at every opportunity. It's who I am, what I do, and what I believe God has called me to. So, what is the problem with all this?

Way back in the late 1960s, Christian rocker Larry Norman wrote the classic song 'Why Should the Devil Have All the Good Music?' It debated why a 'good' person would want to be part of a secular band. I can really relate to that, because similar things have been said to me in the context of my love of movies. 'What's a good person like you doing sitting in a cinema, watching *that*?'

To be fair, the question has changed over the years. Not so long ago it was thought by some followers of Christ that Christians shouldn't actually go to the cinema at all (many felt it was OK to have a TV though). It was considered worldly and corrupting. Thank goodness that attitude has mainly vanished into the ether, although it's been replaced with an even more challenging question: are there certain films that Christians shouldn't watch? As a Christian and a film lover, my answer to that question is… well, frankly, yes and no!

Of course, there are some films Christians shouldn't watch. Pornographic material is the obvious place to start. That's out, and there is no need to go any further on that point. But what about horror films, supernatural chillers, and thrillers about people having affairs or dealing drugs? What about 18-certificate films where the language is going to be ripe, the love scenes vivid, and the violence gory, at best?

I turned eighteen in 1980, and if my memory serves, the first 18-certificate film I saw at the cinema was *Alien*, which came out in 1979, so it must have been a reissue.

Alternatively, it might have been *An American Werewolf in London*, which was released in 1981. Whichever it was, both remain on my list of all-time top-ten films. Yes, both have gory scenes. (Whatever you do, don't remind my mum about *that* scene in *Alien* (1979). She saw it on TV and still had nightmares for weeks after!) Both are horror films. But I find them incredibly entertaining, thrilling and scary. These are classics that I can watch over and over again.

Something I can't (and won't) do, however, is get on a roller-coaster. Honestly, just the thought makes me shudder. Why people want to get on one of those things and risk, at the very most life and limb, and at the least being ill, is totally beyond me. (I did once manage the old Thunder Mountain ride at Disneyland and considered myself a hero, but that was the limit.) Roller-coasters are just way too scary. So why do people line up, hoping to get a seat in the front carriage? Because they want the thrills, chills and experience.

Human beings like being scared. My way of experiencing thrills and chills is to sit through a horror or science-fiction movie. It can be a deeply uncomfortable and unsettling experience, but it gets the blood pumping, and it does feel… exhilarating. I love it in the same way that other people love sitting on a roller-coaster.

The moment that seagull pecks Tippi Hedren on the head in *The Birds* (1963); the sight of the bathroom door opening in *Psycho* (1960); watching John Hurt have his final meal in *Alien* (1979); seeing Frankenstein rise from his slab (*Frankenstein*, 1931); hearing Jenny Agutter scream as the werewolf dies in *An American Werewolf in London*

(1981) – these all have the same effect… and somehow, because it's only a movie, it isn't bad. At least I'm not about to get thrown from a moving train into a funfair at high speed!

Horror films, science-fiction films, and chilling films remind us that we are human. They remind us that there is evil in the world, that the supernatural is real, and that humanity's capacity for evil is greater than we realise. They scare us because this horror might actually be possible. Yet at the same time they also help us – they help *me* – to remember that when everything goes to pot, and life isn't as it should be, I am on the winning side, regardless. Jesus is coming again, the devil will be defeated, and heaven awaits believers.

In the vast majority of horror films, evil is eventually defeated. Good (God in some shape or form) always wins. Justice is done and the evil spirit, alien or mad scientist is done away with. The message of *The Exorcist* (1974) is that self-sacrifice and love beat even the devil himself – check it out. My favourite line in any supernatural horror film occurs towards the end of *The Devil's Advocate* (1990). Kevin Lomax (Keanu Reeves) is talking to his dad, John Milton (Al Pacino), who happens to be the devil incarnate. Keanu tells his dad that he has read the Bible and that the good book tells him they are destined to lose. This was a punch-the-air moment in a horror film for me. (Did you know that *The Exorcist* was banned in the Communist Bloc for being too pro-Christianity? Christ always wins!)

So when I watch and enjoy these films as a Christian, I can do so secure in the knowledge that I am not only on the winning side but that all will be well. However, some consider this argument a cop-out, and see no justification for watching such films. After all, there is an old Christian chorus called 'O Be Careful, Little Eyes' that warns us to take care about what we expose ourselves to. This is a valid point, and if you feel like horror, science-fiction or supernatural films compromise your faith, don't watch them. But I enjoy them for the reasons outlined above, and I watch them, as a Christian, knowing they always remind me that everything will be all right in the end.

However, there is another aspect to this. Many years ago, I found myself working at an event where the speaker was one Mary Whitehouse, considered by many as the nation's moral guardian back then. She was the founder and president of the National Viewers' and Listeners' Association, which spoke out against immorality, violence and unseemly behaviour on TV and on film. Now, just to be clear, I didn't always agree with all her arguments, but I have always remembered one thing she said that evening, and it was this (I may be paraphrasing, it was a while ago): 'I have never complained about anything that I have not seen.' Good on you, Mary. Absolutely right.

At the end of the event, as we stewards were cleaning up, Mary graciously came over to thank us for our work, and I had the opportunity to ask her about what she had said. 'Oh yes,' she said. 'How can you comment on something you haven't seen?'

She is so right. You can't. As my friend and fellow film critic Mark Kermode says, 'Never review anything you haven't seen!'

So here is another reason (and no it's not a cop-out) for watching some of these films. Having seen them, I am able to comment on and review them. I am able to discuss them. I also have the right to complain about them if I feel the need to, and sometimes I do. As someone who writes film reviews, I am able to advise fellow viewers on the content of films and say whether I think they are any good or should be avoided. I can't do that if I haven't seen them.

But… There's that word again. But am I not encouraging people to watch this kind of film, and isn't there proof that watching such films leads to 'copycat' behaviour? Isn't it possible that watching a film about the occult could lead people into the occult? Doesn't violence beget violence? Aren't I in danger of leading some astray?

Of course, all of the above is possible, and it's tragic when these things happen. Therefore, the warning comes to all – don't watch these films if you don't think you can handle them. Don't watch if you are easily influenced. Don't go to see them if they are likely to give you nightmares. Stay away if you fear that such films might affect your behaviour in any way whatsoever.

Those of us who are Christians are told to watch over, watch out for and pray for one another. If we notice that someone appears to be getting hooked on or becoming unduly influenced by something – be it films, drugs, porn or something else – we have a responsibility to take action. We can do this by boycotting films, writing to our MP, and speaking out and encouraging others to do the same. Something Christians don't do enough. Generally speaking, only in the most extreme cases would watching a film affect people's behaviour or change their mindset, but we should always be on our guard for ourselves and for others.

As Christians, our standards should be the very highest, and we each have to make up our own minds about our limits and limitations. We have to decide what is right for us to watch, and what isn't. I am certainly not going to judge you for any position you may take. You answer to the Lord – as I do.

I know some Christian parents who were appalled by the wizarding world of *Harry Potter* (2001-2011) but were happy for their children to watch *Snow White* (1938) or *The Wizard of Oz* (1939). It really is up to you (and if you're a Christian, it's between you and God). Yes, both *Alien* and *An American Werewolf in London* are on my top-ten films list. Yes, I've seen *The Exorcist*, and yes, I will probably go to see the next big supernatural blockbuster, but at least I'll be able to tell you about it from a place of knowledge.

Thank you, Mary Whitehouse, for confirming what I believe to be true. After all, why should the devil have all the good movies?

Intermission 1
All Is Vanity (2021)

Director: Marcos Mereles
Starring: Sid Phoenix, Yaseen Aroussi, Isabelle Bonfrer, Rosie Steel and Christopher Sherwood

While this is an intimate film with a small cast in a limited location – a film studio in London – it gives you a lot to think about. On the face of it, it's a film about a model being photographed for a magazine, which then becomes something else, and then something else. It is a bit like a Russian doll; every new scene changes the story and what you think you know. The ever-changing nature of this short film means you have to concentrate, but it does manage to continually surprise.

The cast is great, each member playing their role with conviction, and the script provides ample opportunities for them to stretch their acting muscles. The Argentinean director, Marcos Mereles, also wrote and produced the film. *All Is Vanity* made for a very confident and self-assured debut, and I look forward to what Mereles has in store for us next.

2
Science-fiction double feature

Does anyone else remember those heady days of the double feature? That's right, younger readers, there was a time when you could go to see two films for the price of one. How about that? I don't remember going to many, but I did attend a few, and they do still happen today. The first I recall seeing was *Escape from the Planet of the Apes* (1971), which was shown as a double bill with the first in the series when it was released. The first film was called… er… *Planet of the Apes* (1968).

I remember spending another great evening watching a double bill of John Carpenter's *The Fog* (1980) teamed with *Alien*. And on 11 October 2015, I saw all three *Back to the Future* films (1985-90) back-to-back, as that was the day Marty McFly famously arrived in the future.

You will probably have noticed that the one thing these films have in common is that they are all science-fiction films (well, *The Fog* aside). I love sci-fi movies and always have done. My dad liked them as well. I remember as a youngster watching such classics as *Village of the Damned* (1960), *The Day of the Triffids* (1963), *This Island Earth* (1955), *The Day the Earth Stood Still* (1951) and *The Incredible Shrinking Man* (1957). (After watching Scott Carey, brilliantly played by Grant Williams, grow smaller and smaller, I was checking my height for weeks.)

I was enthralled by the incredible possibilities these films offered, the thought of how clever humans are, the chance to explore space, and the possibility that we may not be alone. Later, I would fall in love with such films as *Close Encounters of the Third Kind* (1977), *E.T.* (1982), *Independence Day* (1996), *Men in Black* (1997), *Arrival* (2016), *Inception* (2010) – and of course, as anyone who knows me knows, my beloved *Star Trek* in all its many forms. Boldly going where no man – sorry – no *one* – has gone before was the most exhilarating experience imaginable, and the fact that the characters on the USS *Enterprise* were all such great company was an added bonus. I confess that when I went to see *Star Trek III: The Search for Spock* (1984 – I was at the first public showing in the UK), I wept my heart out when the *Enterprise* was destroyed. Heck, I grew up on that ship!

Aliens, of course, come in all sorts of shapes and sizes. There are the big, ugly monsters that are out to get us and want our planet for their own. Then there are the friendlier, more intellectual creatures that just want to communicate and be friendly. They sometimes teach us lessons about ourselves, and at other times we are to learn from them directly. If only we had been prepared to listen to Klaatu in *The Day the Earth Stood Still* (2008) instead of shooting him within seconds of him emerging from his ship. If only we hadn't hounded *E.T.* (1982) he might not have had to die, and if we'd been prepared to learn from the aliens in *Contact* (1997), who knows how far we might have travelled. It's not in the film, but in the novel of *2001: A Space Odyssey* (oh, how my family hated that 1968 movie – they've probably all stopped reading this by now), the space child starts dismantling nuclear weapons in orbit around the earth. We even learn that some aliens are subordinate to the smallest things on Earth, such as when bacteria wipes out the invaders from Mars.

I honestly don't feel it's too much of an exaggeration to say that science-fiction films have an awful lot to reveal about the human condition. The tagline for *Star Trek: The Motion Picture* (1979) told that our human adventure was just beginning. Data, the android in *Star Trek: The Next Generation* (1987), longs to be human and is often taught lessons about the value of human existence. Even the murderous replicant Roy Batty in *Blade Runner* (1982) only wants more life.

Logan's Run (1976) presents a world in which people are not allowed to die old, and many films show us that a world in which humans are replaced with mechanoids is not a nice place to live. *Silent Running* (1972) teaches us about the value of preserving our beautiful planet, while films like *Metropolis* (1927) and *District 9* (2009) carry the not-so-subtle message that we are all equal and should treat everyone the same way. Many other films show us what can be achieved when we all pull together – stand up *Independence Day* (1996). So many lessons to learn, so little time – unless you happen to have a spare DeLorean and know a mad, yet helpful, scientist.

One film I mentioned above that I have vivid memories of seeing for the first time is *E.T.* I was at theological college at the time, and a group of us went to see it. During the scene when E.T. 'dies', I distinctly remember hearing sobbing coming from all around the auditorium. This tender moment was broken when one of my fellow students whispered, 'It's only a lump of plastic, for Pete's sake!' Talk about ruining a moment.

After that, I lost count of the number of children's talks based on the film I heard in churches. After all, E.T. came from the heavens, died, rose again, and told us to behave and be nice, and then went back to the heavens. Remind you of anyone?

Not only do sci-fi films have a great deal to say about the human condition, but they also force us to ask questions about the nature of existence, creation and the fate of the universe. They present the possibility of life elsewhere, and force us to explore what we are doing to improve ourselves. We either go down the *Star Trek* route to a united Earth or down the road that leads to us blowing up the planet and letting the apes take our place. We can either embrace the aliens or let them take over... and maybe destroy us all in the process. The choice, it seems, is ours.

The Bible has a great deal to say about humanity, and, believe it or not, most of it is positive. We are created in the image of God – imagine that! We have eternal souls and a God who wants us to spend eternity with him in paradise. The Bible talks about our potential to achieve great things and to go to great places. Music, craft, work, marriage, technology, medicine, imagination, love, education and sex were all God's ideas, and they are all incredibly magnificent ideas. In addition, God gave us this wonderful, beautiful, amazing planet to live on, and enabled us to do all these things.

No, the Bible doesn't answer all our questions – neither does it tell us if there is indeed life on other planets. (I confess that I would love to know and, maybe controversially, remain open to the idea.) If the Bible doesn't tell me something, I have to conclude that a) I don't need to know; b) It's actually not that important; and c) These things are best left to God.

What is important is that God loves human beings, and he loves us so much that he planned for us to spend eternity with him. That's fantastic. The problem is not with God's plan or design; it is that *we* messed up. We turned our backs on him, became disobedient, and felt that we could do better without him. We clearly can't. So God sent Jesus to sort out the mess we made. He paid the cost for it all on the cross, rose again, and now says that everything can be set right if we simply trust in him.

One of my favourite science-fiction franchises of all time is, without a doubt, *The X-Files*, which spawned two movies (1998; 2008). I loved following FBI special agents Mulder and Scully as they investigated the supernatural, the paranormal and the possibility of alien existence. The show was thrilling, complex and a sheer delight for fans of the genre. The tagline for the show, as you may recall, was: 'The truth is out there.' If science fiction teaches us anything, it is that the search for truth goes on and on. If the Bible teaches us anything, it is that we need look no further than Jesus Christ if we want the truth. He told it, lived it and *is* it. The search is over and the human adventure, which is just beginning, can be an eternal one if we trust in him. So, let's boldly go…

Intermission 2
Anatomy of a Fall (2023)

Director: Justine Triet
Starring: Sandra Huller. Swann Arlaud. Milon Machado-Graner. Antoine Reinartz

Did she or didn't she? That's the question at the heart of this good, if not great, courtroom drama. Did Sandra kill her husband, Samuel, or didn't she?

Sandra and Samuel are writers who frequently argue about their work. Sandra's latest novel was a major success, but Samuel is angry with her for stealing his ideas. They live in a beautiful Alpine home with their partially blind eleven-year-old son, when one day Samuel is found dead, having fallen from a third-floor balcony. Sandra is the only other person in the house and ends up being tried for his murder.

This film not only provides a courtroom drama, but takes a forensic look at a marriage and a family falling apart. It features good performances from all the lead characters, supported by a clever script and a lovely score.

Anatomy of a Fall is an incredibly beautiful movie, set in some of the most scenic parts of France, from the Auvergne-Rhône-Alpes to Paris. What spoilt it for me, however, is that it was too long (around two-and-a-half hours), and the final half-hour dragged once the jury had delivered its verdict. That said, the film was a major hit with the majority of critics and won a host of awards at film festivals all over the world – including Film of the Year from the London Film Critics' Circle and the Palme d'Or at the Cannes Film Festival. It also won the Oscar for Best Original Screenplay in 2024.

A good, solid whodunnit that many will enjoy.

3
Do you hear the people sing?

You should do, because apparently the hills are alive with the sound of music – and even if it's raining, someone, somewhere will be singing in it. The musical movie has always been with us and always will be. Indeed, the first-ever talkie (*The Jazz Singer*, 1927) was a musical, and one of its stars, Al Jolson, was proved right when he proclaimed that we hadn't heard anything yet. Since that moment the musical has never gone away, and I have to say that I, for one, am very, very happy about that. I love them. And the fact that my musical taste is so eclectic means I really can't think of a musical I don't like.

Although the musical has always been with us, there has been a real resurgence of this wonderful form of entertainment in recent years. Films like *Rocketman*, *Yesterday*, *Wild Rose*, *Anna and the Apocalypse* and others have helped a new generation to discover the joy of watching people sing, dance and tell their stories to music.

My own personal favourite of recent times, and in fact a film that sits in my list of all-time top-five movies (honestly) is the magnificent, sensational and utterly brilliant *La La Land* (2016 – other opinions are available, of course… but they're wrong!). It's a film that pays tribute to the golden era of Hollywood, owing much to films like *The Band Wagon* (1953) and *Singin' in the Rain* (1952), and which deservedly won six Oscars, even if it was robbed of the award for Best Picture in arguably the most famous moment in Oscar history. Those who were watching that night will never forget Warren Beatty and Faye Dunaway announcing that *La La Land* had won the award, when in fact the real winner was the rather dour melodrama *Moonlight* (2016).

In-between *The Jazz Singer* and *La La Land*, there have been so many musicals that it would take a whole book – a very big book – to document them all. You can find films to cover all musical tastes from classical to rock, and they cover all sorts of topics as well: everything from love to fame, war to revolution, poverty to riches, coping with disability and death to the supernatural. There have even been musicals about creatures from outer space – take a bow, *Little Shop of Horrors* (1986).

Every emotion is laid bare in musicals. Love, jealousy, hatred, concern – the full gauntlet is run, and the vain ambition and crazy antics of the protagonists often hold us in thrall. We often find ourselves rooting for them and wishing them well in their endeavours. We share their joy and pain as they express themselves in song – a medium that has a way of touching our hearts and pulling at the strings attached to them in ways that the spoken word rarely can.

When Fantine (Anne Hathaway) sings of the dreams she used to dream, but which are now shattered (*Les Misérables*, 2012) we find ourselves weeping with her; when Kathy, Don and Cosmo (Debbie Reynolds, Gene Kelly and Donald O'Connor) see in the morning after a disastrous night (*Singin' in the Rain*, 1952), we find ourselves praying for success to come their way; when Pardner (Clint Eastwood) starts singing 'I Talk to the Trees' (*Paint Your Wagon*, 1969), we share his wonder at nature and his heartache at the way life is going. We end up desperately hoping that, on some enchanted evening, Nellie (Mitzi Gaynor, *South Pacific*, 1958) will indeed find her true love. Tevye (Topol) shares all the things he would do if he were a rich man (*Fiddler on the Roof*, 1971), and we hope his dreams come true. When Eliza Doolittle (Audrey Hepburn) is finally able to proclaim that the rain in Spain really does fall on the plain to the satisfaction of Professor Higgins (Rex Harrison, *My Fair Lady*, 1964), we share in her triumph. When Jack (Himesh Patel) belts out a version of 'Help' that clearly emerges from the very depths of his heart (*Yesterday*, 2019), we feel his pain. And when the 'misfits' of P. T. Barnum's circus belt out 'This Is Me' (*The Greatest Showman*, 2017), we stand and yell, "Oh YES!'

Musicals have the capacity to make us laugh, cry, suffer heartache, fall in love, fall out of love, get angry, and get up and dance. They have the ability to stir us, shake us (and rattle and roll us!), as well as making us feel emotions that may take us by surprise. I vividly remember crying at the death of Tony in *West Side Story* (1961), laughing out loud at Danny's (John Travolta's) reaction to Sandy's (Olivia Newton-John's) transformation in *Grease* (1978), and feeling stunned as a drunk Norman (James Mason) expressed his complete and utter jealousy of his wife's newfound fame in *A Star is Born* (1954).

The release of emotions is of course no bad thing. How often have we been told that bottling things up is not good for us? It's good to let it all out, and one of the best ways to do that, and to express ourselves, is in song.

This is one reason why I love the Bible's very own songbook so much. The book of Psalms contains 150 songs that cover every subject you could possibly think of. The writers sing about love, hatred, depression, broken relationships, adultery, murder, human nature and the existence of God. They sing about their hopes, doubts, fears, dreams, successes and joys. These songs are honest, down-to-earth and utterly relevant. If you need material for a good musical, look no further than the efforts of these gifted, talented and inspired lyricists.

They aren't all depressing, as some have suggested. The writers spend a great deal of time talking about the good things in their lives as well as praising God for his goodness to them. They express all the things I want to say but probably wouldn't be able to find the words for. When I find prayer or praise difficult, I can always open up the book of Psalms and use their words instead. They say what I want to say, only much more eloquently.

The next time you find yourself wanting to express your feelings – sadness, joy, depression, anxiety, praise or gratitude – work your way through this fantastic collection of songs, and I guarantee – yes, I *guarantee* – you will find something that fits your mood exactly.

There is no way I could end this chapter without further reference to my favourite musical of all time, *Les Misérables*. I'm not referring to the movie version (2012), which in my opinion got it all wrong (it had the same director who later made the ill-fated movie version of *Cats* in 2019, so maybe we shouldn't be surprised), but I have seen it on stage in London's West End a number of times, and was very fortunate to be taken by good friends to see the staged concert version in 2019. On stage that night were Alfie Boe, Michael Ball and Matt Lucas – and I can honestly say that it was one of the greatest nights of my life. The compelling story is told with music and lyrics that are overwhelming, powerful and breathtaking. I adore the tunes, melodies, lyrics and majesty of the show.

It was such a shame that the film version really messed things up. As noted above, Anne Hathaway was fine, but the rest of the film was badly miscast. Russell Crowe only proved that he couldn't sing, songs were placed out of order – and worse, edited (it was criminal what they did to 'Beggars at the Feast') – and a totally pointless new song was added. I think you have probably gathered by now that I really don't like the film, but boy do I love the stage show.

Les Misérables is a story about redemption, forgiveness, hope and love. In its most climactic moment, our hero, facing his own death, asks God to forgive his sins and take him home to glory. He is then assured by the spirts of the departed Fantine and Éponine that he will indeed see God's face; that even for the most wretched there is hope; that hope comes through faith and belief. I, for one, am looking forward to all that the God of heaven has in store for me when I go to be with him in glory.

Intermission 3
Black Panther: Wakanda Forever (2022)

Director: Ryan Coolger
Starring: Chadwick Boseman. Michael B. Jordan. Lupita Nyong'o. Danal Gurira

Alfred Hitchcock once suggested that the length of a film should equate to the capacity of the human bladder. Knowing that this new Marvel epic was nearly three hours long – including a sequence midway through the end credits – I had very little to drink going into it!

The question over a film's length has long been debated by movie fans and Hitchcock certainly had a point. But think about it for a moment. *Gone with the Wind* (1939) and *Ben-Hur* (1959) came in at just under four hours, while *Psycho* (1960) and *Toy Story* (1995) were both less than two hours. Would you want to lose a minute of any of those? Absolutely not!

As long as the film tells its story, has a gripping opening, a sustained and engrossing middle, and a satisfying conclusion, who cares how long it is? It's the films that drag on and have completely unnecessary subplots and 'character-driven' scenes that seem to take an eternity that I struggle with. There are times when I just want to yell at the screen, 'For Pete's sake, just get on with it!'

This brings me back to the latest Marvel epic, which kind of falls in the middle category. There were moments when I was enjoying myself so much and was so invested in what was unfolding that I didn't even think about looking at my watch. However, at other times during its lengthy running time I sat back in my chair, thinking, *Come on, move it along.* Why does every battle scene have to be in slow motion? Seriously, why?

In this film, Wakanda comes under attack from another mythical kingdom of undersea dwellers and the characters in both kingdoms are well fleshed out. One of the unnecessary subplots involves us ordinary humans looking on and trying to get involved when it's really none of our business. Martin Freeman is wasted in that regard.

The film is dedicated to Chadwick Boseman, a great actor who played the Black Panther back in 2018 and was set to star in the sequel. Sadly, he passed away in 2020 aged just forty-three. His untimely death meant scenes that had already been filmed had to be scrapped and the story changed to incorporate the death of his character. This probably explains why the story is a bit rambling and at times elongated. But it's a fitting tribute, nonetheless. You can tell that the entire cast is genuinely cut up about the death of their fellow star. It's as if when the script talks about 'the king's' death it's actually talking about Chadwick's.

The action is spectacular, undercut with a beautiful score (there is a lovely song by Rihanna called 'Lift Me Up' that plays over the end credits, which is worth staying for).

The first film was just over two hours long, so with this one being much longer I guess you could say that you get value for money. That said, boy did I need a drink – and the loo – by the time it was over.

4
The Name's Godfrey... Andy Godfrey

Hey, I can dream, can't I? The pop group Scouting for Girls had the same dream. They wished they could be James Bond, dealing with the baddie and getting the girl. I don't play video games, but I'm told that some of the James Bond games allow you to do just that. Maybe I need to buy a console.

The Bond franchise is of course the longest-running and most successful in the movie world, and while we wait for the next Bond to be named, we have twenty-five existing Bond adventures to keep us going.

It is interesting that the character we see portrayed in the films is often very different from the morose, depressed, introverted character created by Ian Fleming; a man who often despises what he has to do but gets on with it anyway. This is why I prefer the films that more accurately depict the Bond of the books. For me, the very best films in the series are those that have fewer fanciful elements, and are more down-to-earth and realistic. I love *Skyfall* (2012), *Spectre* (2015), *From Russia With Love* (1963) and *A Licence to Kill* (1989).

The worst for me is unquestionably the silly, over-the-top and totally nonsensical *Moonraker* (1979; good song, though – and a third for Shirley Bassey). Of the Roger Moore outings, I like *For Your Eyes Only* (1981) best. It's interesting that they made this after *Moonraker* and reverted to Bond using only his ingenuity rather than relying on gadgets and fast cars.

My personal favourite Bond, Daniel Craig, may have been criticised when he got the role for having the wrong hair colour, but he has gone on to embody Bond and make him his own. I was very sorry to see him move on.

The very first Bond film I saw at the cinema was Roger Moore's third outing as Bond in *The Spy Who Loved Me* (1977). It was also the very first soundtrack album I ever bought. It was notable for a number of reasons – not least the fact that it featured the biggest soundstage ever constructed at Pinewood. Built to house three full-sized nuclear submarines, the action was certainly spectacular and gripping. The film also introduced the character of Jaws, with his shining metal teeth, and had one of the very best pre-credit sequences of them all, in which Bond skies off the side of a mountain. The title song (well, the official title is 'Nobody Does It Better') was a big hit, and one of the most memorable of the series.

The film started my love affair with Bond, but also drove me to read the original novels. Here I began to notice a few differences. Did you know that *The Spy Who Loved Me* is actually a short story set in a snowbound hotel in America? Or that it is narrated by a female character who is trapped in the hotel with a load of gangsters? Enter Bond... A bit different, right?

Daniel Craig may be my favourite Bond – I believe he embodies the Bond of the books perfectly – however, my favourite Bond film, and indeed Bond novel, is *On Her Majesty's Secret Service* (1969). I will explain in the next chapter why it's also one of my favourite Christmas movies (honestly!).

With Sean Connery tiring of the role, a new Bond was unveiled to the world in *On Her Majesty's Secret Service*. Unknown Australian actor George Lazenby was introduced as the new 007 – and, depending on your point of view, was either terrible, wooden and useless, or excellent, well cast and a great Bond. I hold the latter view. Actually, for a large chunk of the film Lazenby has to play Bond playing someone else – the rather prissy, fussy and non-adventurous Sir Hilary Bray. Somehow, I can't imagine Connery in that role. The film has some great stunts, beautiful locations, the wonderful Diana Rigg, and a great storyline. Also, arguably the best score of the whole series. Many Bond fans agree with me about both Lazenby and the film score. As an aside, if you ever get the chance to visit Piz Gloria (the Swiss ski resort where some of the movie was filmed), do. It's magnificent.

The film certainly features one of the most audacious moments in the entire franchise. Right at the start, a young woman runs away from Bond. He looks directly into the camera and refers to the fact that this sort of thing never happened to his predecessor. I had the privilege of meeting George, and he told me that this line was his idea; however, if you listen to the director's commentary track on the Blu-ray, Peter Hunt says he thought of it. Either way, it was an excellent way to introduce the new Bond. It's just a shame that Lazenby never went on to make more, as I believe he really could have established himself in the role.

Secret agents and spies have been with us almost since the dawn of cinema, and while Bond may still be the most popular, others have arisen to challenge him: Jason Bourne, Kingsman and Ethan Hunt (the *Mission Impossible* series, which began in 1996) among them. I think we could also add Jack Bauer to that list, although *24* is of course TV.

However, the death of Tracy, who had only just become Mrs Bond in *On Her Majesty's Secret Service*, is no longer the most shocking moment in the Bond series. For that, we had to wait till 2021 and the twenty-fifth film in the series. I will always remember receiving a call from my brother after he had been to see *No Time to Die*. He simply said, 'They can't *do* that!' But they had…

He was referring to the fact that Bond – yes, James Bond – dies at the end of that film. By the time my brother saw it, I had already done so three times and had accepted the fact that the great hero was gone. However, most people, like my brother, were stunned.

But it's not as if our heroes haven't died before. Captain Kirk dies in *Star Trek: Generations* (1994). Hans Solo dies in *Star Wars: The Force Awakens* (2015) and even Superman meets his end in *Batman v Superman: Dawn of Justice* (2016). Superman aside, these men are only human, and death is a reality we all must face – no matter who we are.

Spies like Bond are dedicated, talented, brave, courageous, irresistible to the opposite sex, well-paid and intelligent, and have a never-say-die attitude that always gets them through the most horrendous of circumstances. But they are also only human. They can be vulnerable as well – they do have hearts, and their hearts can be broken. Nevertheless, many of us, like Scouting for Girls have wished we could be James Bond for a day.

For the majority, becoming an international man (or woman) of mystery is just a dream. However, Christianity teaches us that God has an important plan and purpose for each of us. If you like, he is the ultimate M. He has stuff he wants us to do, and he puts us in the right places to do it. He gives us the gadgets – the tools and gifts we need to fulfil his plan – and his Q – the Holy Spirit – sticks with us to see the job through.

I will never be James Bond, but I can be the person God made me to be simply by trusting him and getting on with the job – however odd it may appear to be. My job is full-time evangelism. What's yours? Let's all look forward to the day when we hear the Lord say, 'Well done, good and faithful servant!' (Matthew 25:23). Or in spy speak, 'Mission accomplished!'

Intermission 4
Eiffel (2021)

Director: Martin Bourboulon
Starring: Romain Duris, Emma Mackay

'Freely inspired by real facts,' director Martin Bourboulon's film provides a delightful diversion. It gives us an interesting look at the life of the man who, according to this film, had two real loves in his life: the famous Parisian tower and the daughter of a well-to-do family with whom he had an on-off romance for many years. Her name was Adriene, and the film would have us believe that the shape of the tower has something to do with the first letter of her name.

This rather charming movie provides a nice change of pace from recent blockbusters, but don't be fooled. The romance story is purely fictional, while the scenes documenting the construction of the tower are based on fact. Gustave Eiffel had to jump through so many hoops to get it finished, and it is testament to his dogged determination that it stands to this day. Problems with soggy ground meant special devices had to be constructed to get the foundations right. And at times he ran out of money and had to cope with workers going on strike.

Romain Duris, who plays Eiffel, puts in a great performance as a man on a mission, and Emma Mackey is very affecting as the love interest. If I had to pick fault with the film, it would be with the ending. The final scenes feel very rushed, and I'd liked to have learned a little more about the actual work done to finish the tower, as much of the time is spent telling us how they got up to level one.

Despite this, a delightful score by Alexandre Desplat moves things along nicely, and all in all this is a very pleasant, and in part educational, experience.

5
I'm dreaming of a movie-filled Christmas

I wonder if any other movie fans remember the days when you couldn't wait for the TV listing magazine to arrive. You would quickly snap it up and begin ticking off the films you wanted to see. Bond after Christmas dinner was always a must for me. These days, the chances are you've seen all the movies on offer and maybe even own them, but there is still nothing like settling down with a full stomach to watch a movie at Christmas.

However, when it comes to the question of what we should watch, opinions can be very divided and not everyone will agree. We each have our favourite Christmas films, but thankfully there is something for everyone. Here are my top Christmas movies – films I simply cannot do without over the festive season. I know you're not going to agree with them all, and I've probably left out your favourite… but that's the fun of film criticism. It would be boring if we all agreed on everything.

10. *Krampus* (2015)
We all know that Father Christmas comes to children who have been nice and good. But what about those who have been naughty? The answer is, they get a visit from Krampus. Based on an ancient German legend, Krampus is a horned creature who leaves chaos in his wake.

Set on Christmas Eve, the film follows a family as they get together for Christmas, not knowing that one of their younger members has stopped believing in the spirit of the season. The film is creepy, funny and scary. It has some great 'jump scares' and a terrific ending that wraps things up beautifully.

9. *On Her Majesty's Secret Service* (1969)
Well, I did say there should always be a Bond film on Christmas Day, but before you start thinking I've lost the plot altogether because the film has little or nothing to do with Christmas, please consider the following. It is set at Christmas and New Year, even Blofed has a Christmas tree.

On Christmas Eve we see Blofeld's 'angels of death' drinking eggnog and opening Christmas presents. Bond and his wife make a dramatic escape and find themselves in a barn (stable?) on Christmas Eve, where Bond proposes. The next day they go skiing, and the climactic battle takes place on New Year's Eve. There is even a delightful song on the soundtrack called 'Do You Know How Christmas Trees Are Grown?'. I rest my case – it's a Christmas movie!

8. *White Christmas* (1954)

What would Christmas be without this perennial classic? Bing Crosby, Rosemary Clooney, Danny Kaye and Vera-Ellen in a timeless story of a successful song-and-dance duo who become romantically involved with a sister act and team up to save the failing Columbia Inn, which belongs to the boys' former commanding general. The highlight, of course, is Bing crooning out the title number, and many people consider this the best Christmas movie ever.

7. *The Nightmare Before Christmas* (1994)

Tim Burton's dark, stop-motion musical fantasy has become a favourite for many, doubling up as both a Halloween and a Christmas movie. Jack Skellington, King of Halloween Town, discovers Christmas Town. Amazed by the lack of monsters, spooks and ghosts, he is completely captivated by the warm feeling he gets from Christmas and decides he wants it for himself.

As well as being great fun, this film has real heart and pathos. The musical numbers are superbly staged, and the story is captivating. The real charm is that even though you know you are watching clay figures being brought to life, you really come to like and care for the characters.

6. *Love Actually* (2003)

This film opens with Bill Nighy singing a great Christmas number and features Hugh Grant as a prime minister we can only dream of having. A stellar British cast shines in this wonderfully comic film, which tells the story of eight very different couples in various loosely related tales during the frantic month before Christmas. This film is funny, charming, wonderful and a delight to watch.

5. *Gremlins* (1984)
When young Billy's dad tells him not to get his new pet wet, expose him to bright light or feed him after midnight, you just know that trouble is on its way. The film takes place on Christmas Eve and is great fun. It's a crazy, chaotic, frantic roller-coaster of a movie, which even makes time for one of the most tear-jerking stories you will witness in any Christmas film. Sit back and enjoy the fun as the gremlins sing Christmas carols and even go to the movies!

4. *It's a Wonderful Life* (1947)
Angel Clarence gets his wings in this timeless classic. One of the most uplifting films ever made, it surely has to be on everyone's list of great Christmas movies. On the verge of committing suicide, George Bailey (played by James Stewart), is shown what a world without him would look like. This film is beautifully judged. Even if you have seen it dozens of times, make sure you have some tissues ready.

3. *A Christmas Carol* (any version)
Alastair Sim, Albert Finney, Patrick Stewart, Jim Carrey, George C. Scott, Mickey Mouse, Jack Palance, Kelsey Grammer, Simon Callow, Bill Murray – take your pick. All these great actors and others have taken on the part of Ebenezer Scrooge in many different interpretations of the story. Genuinely scary dramas, musicals and comedies, they

have all been used to take us into Dickens's world. We all have our favourite versions, but whichever you prefer, you have to have some sort of encounter[1] with Scrooge at Christmas.

2. *Die Hard* (1989)

A few years back, Bruce Willis said that *Die Hard* is not a Christmas movie, to which I and many other film fans responded with, 'Oh, come off it.' Again, consider the evidence. John McClane (played by Bruce) has travelled to L.A. to be reunited with his wife and family on Christmas Eve. He's carrying a massive teddy bear.

Bruce goes on to dispatch a terrorist, dressing him in a Santa hat and writing "Now I have a machine gun, HO-HO-HO" on his T-shirt. Arch-villain Alan Rickman refers to the festive period as a time when miracles take place, and in the last line of the film, limo driver Argyle jokes that if Christmas is this much fun, he had better come back for New Year. Shortly afterwards, Vaughn Monroe starts up with 'Let It Snow! Let It Snow! Let It Snow!' And – oh yes – Mrs McClane's first name is Holly. I rest my case.

1. *The Muppet Christmas Carol* (1992)

Yes, I know we've already mentioned a host of movies based on *A Christmas Carol*, but for me, this one beats the lot and deserves to be singled out. Shortly after Kermit sings 'One More Sleep 'Til Christmas', we witness the transformation of Michael Caine from what Dickens describes in the novel

---

[1] Charles Dickens, *A Christmas Carol* (public domain).

as a 'squeezing, wrenching, grasping, scraping, clutching, a covetous old sinner', whom even the vegetables dislike (a classic line from the movie) to a man who knows how to celebrate Christmas well. This film provides superb entertainment for all ages and is a must-see every year.

So, there you have it – my top-ten Christmas movies. Whatever yours are, enjoy them and, as Tiny Tim observes at the end of the book, 'God bless us, every one' (Dickens, *A Christmas Carol*).

For me, however, the best portrayal of the Christmas story itself – the one involving Mary and Joseph – was not a film shown in cinemas, but a TV series first shown in the UK back in 2010. *The Nativity* is a brilliantly written retelling of the biblical account. It realistically portrayed the impact Mary's divine pregnancy must have had on her, on her family and friends, and on Joseph. When Joseph discovers that Mary is 'with child', we see his anger, frustration and total confusion at what is going on. Mary is branded a whore by the other women of Nazareth and goes to spend time with her cousin Elizabeth in Jerusalem.

I thought the series was extremely well done, wonderfully acted and superbly written. Famously, Tony Jordan started writing the script in 2007. At the time he didn't believe in the Nativity story, but said that, after researching for and writing *The Nativity*, his opinion changed.

I hope you'll check out this series at Christmastime if you haven't already seen it (you can get it on DVD) and rejoice in the reality of what happened that first Christmas. No wonder it's often referred to as the greatest story ever told… Check out the next chapter for more on this theme.

Intermission 5
Rosalie (2023)

Director: Stephanie Di Giusto
Starring: Nadia Tereszkiewicz, Benoit Magimel

So, this could be awkward, but let's not make it so… and just go for it. OK? According to Wikipedia, a freak is 'a person who is physically deformed or transformed due to an extraordinary medical condition or body modification'.[2] The term was originally neutral, simply referring to those who were physically different, but soon came to be used in a pejorative sense.

'Freaks' have featured in a large number of films over the years, often in a circus setting. We don't have time to list them all here, but I could refer you to Tod Browning's controversial 1932 film entitled… er… *Freaks*. It was so

---

[2] 'Freak': https://en.wikipedia.org/wiki/Freak (accessed 6 June 2024).

graphic and horrific that many cinemagoers left, screaming. A classic of the genre, it remains a tough watch. Then we have David Lynch's 1980 classic *The Elephant Man*, with an incredible performance from Sir Anthony Hopkins in the title role. More recently, *The Greatest Showman*, directed by *La La Land's* Damien Chazelle, and based on the life and circus of P. T. Barnum, was a massive worldwide hit.

Now we have *Rosalie*, a beautifully touching, strange and compelling film, loosely based on the life of Clémentine Delait, who lived in Brittany in the 1870s. She is desperate for love, so her father marries her off to a bar owner in a small mining village. However, it's only on their wedding night that her new husband discovers her secret. Her body is covered in hair, and she has a beard that grows so rapidly it becomes very hard to keep it a secret. Trouble ensues!

I have to say that I loved this film. The acting is fantastic and the story deeply moving. Again, you may have to hunt it down to watch it, but it'll be more than worth your time. The film is a powerful reminder that God loves and accepts us all, whatever we look like.

6
Let there be lights, camera, action!
(A history of the Bible on film)

Ever since the very early days of cinema, one book has provided inspiration, stories and plenty of action for filmmakers. Apart from being the world's bestseller, this book contains every kind of story imaginable. There are battles, romances, miracles, supernatural events and heroes of every kind. That book is of course the Bible, and literally hundreds of movies have been made from the stories it tells.

Almost every story in the Bible has been filmed at some point or another since 1903. From *Adam and Eve* (1912) right through to Mel Gibson's *The Passion of the Christ: Resurrection* (no release date set at the time of writing), the Good Book has been a great source of inspiration for filmmakers everywhere.

Ask most film fans to name a film based on the Bible and they will probably mention *The Ten Commandments*, filmed twice by Cecil B. DeMille (1923; 1956); *Samson and Delilah* (1949), also directed by DeMille and starring Hedy Lamar and Victor Mature; Mel Gibson's *The Passion of the Christ* (2004); Ridley Scott's *Exodus: Gods and Kings* (2014); and Darren Aronofsky's rather entertaining but very unbiblical retelling of *Noah* (2014).

However, perhaps the most ambitious project ever relating to the Bible appeared in 1966. It was announced that the whole of the Old Testament was going to be filmed, with director John Huston at the helm. In the end he only managed to film the first twenty-two chapters of Genesis, but with spectacular results. *The Bible: In the Beginning* won many international awards, including an Oscar for Best Original Score.

Some filmmakers have decided it's OK to take liberties with the Bible story and have fun with it, most notably Monty Python. When *Life of Brian* came out in 1979, the uproar was staggering. Deemed blasphemous by many, the film was banned in parts of the UK and met with much international condemnation. Others saw it as a comedy classic. When I asked Mark Kermode for his take, he said, 'That film shows what happens when religion gets out of hand.' It's hard not to agree with him.

Eventually, two of the film's stars and writers, John Cleese and Michael Palin, went on a late-night chat show in order to defend the film. In a famous confrontation, they came up against journalist Malcolm Muggeridge and the then Bishop of Southwark Mervyn Stockwood, both of whom ultimately proved very poor at defending the

Christian faith. Go back and watch the interview again, and you will see that Cleese and Palin not only win the day but are disappointed that it doesn't turn into a serious discussion on the points they made. Both are clear that they are in no way trying to ridicule Christ – in fact, they had abandoned an earlier attempt to do so. It is my opinion that Christ remains impossible to criticise and make fun of, simply because of who and what he is.

If you are keen to see the whole of the Bible on screen, then look no further than an epic miniseries simply called *The Bible*, which was first shown on the History Channel in 2013 and is now available on DVD. The series starts with Genesis and takes you right through the Bible to its conclusion in Revelation.

Other films worthy of a mention are *The Greatest Story Ever Told* (1965); *King of Kings* (1961); *The Prince of Egypt* (1998); *The Gospel According to St. Matthew* (1964); and the stunningly beautiful puppet film *The Miracle Maker* (1999). All these are worth checking out, as they vividly bring the various Bible stories to life in incredibly dramatic ways.

Regardless of the way these biblical stories have been portrayed, the fact is that the Bible is more than just a source of great material for filmmakers. As a Christian, I believe it to be true, and that in the risen Jesus we have all that we need. And what do we need? Friendship, love, peace and assurance, and a certainty that we have a future; that we can be made right with God. So many films end with the words 'Based on a true story', and that could certainly apply to all the films mentioned here.

Intermission 6
Elvis (2022)

Director: Baz Luhrmann
Starring: Austin Butler, Tom Hanks

I wrote this review after returning from a press screening at the Cineworld Leicester Square IMAX, and I'm just going to come out and say it… As I left the building, I was 'all shook up'!

In much the same way Rocketman (2019) used Elton John's music to tell his story (regardless of the order the songs were released), Luhrmann uses Elvis's. But it's not just Elvis's story he's telling. This is as much a film about the 'colonel' (played by Tom Hanks) as it is about Elvis. Both are brilliantly played, and at times I wasn't sure if I was watching Austin Butler (who plays Elvis) or documentary footage! The performance of the classics is top-notch, and looking at the end credits many of the songs are genuine Elvis performances.

The placement of songs at certain points in the story serves to highlight the problems and difficulties Elvis faced. For example, 'Caught in a Trap' plays when Colonel Tom signs a deal behind Elvis's back that prevents him from undertaking his world tour.

As you would expect, Hanks is wonderful as the colonel. One minute he's the kind old uncle who only has the star's best interests at heart, the next he's the wicked, scheming, money-grabbing old codger who held Elvis back. The relationship between the two is dramatically and powerfully portrayed. Stay for the end credits to find out how the colonel ended his days!

In fact, stay for the end credits because the music is wonderful. There are comparisons to be made between this, Rocketman, Judy (2019) and Bohemian Rhapsody (2018). In each case we see people with incredible talent whose lives were be shaped by others whose motives weren't exactly selfless.

Even if you didn't know this was a Baz Luhrsmann film going in, you are left in no doubt within minutes. The telltale signs are all there: the sweeping camera moves, the lavish sets and costumes, the on-screen titles in varying fonts, the spilt screens and the overlapping scenes with the past and present intermingling.

I certainly didn't get the blues, and although we left Elvis in Heartbreak Hotel, there was a part of me that wanted to just shout 'Glory, glory hallelujah'!

7
Making it up as we go along

If, as they say, life begins at forty, just imagine how many more incredible adventures Indiana Jones has ahead of him. It wasn't so long ago that Dr Jones celebrated his fortieth birthday – no, I can't believe it either!

Just to be clear, *Raiders of the Lost Ark* (1981) is the greatest movie ever made. Bar none. No exceptions. Trust me on this, as Indy might say. I saw the film during the week of its initial release in the UK, and there has hardly been a day since when I haven't thought about it, quoted from it or had the fantastic John Williams theme tune running around in my head. There is a large copy of the cinema poster on my front-room wall. I've even met and spoken to two stars of the film.

A few years back I got to interview John Rhys-Davies, who played Indy's sidekick Sallah and was at that time starring in a new version of *The Pilgrim's Progress* (2019). I told him *Raiders* was my favourite film of all time, and when he quoted the line from the film about asps being very dangerous and that Indy should go first into the Well of Souls, a shiver ran down my spine and my hair stood on end. It was an amazing moment.

Better still was the moment when I got to meet the extremely lovely Karen Allen (Marion Ravenwood in the film, and Indy's future wife) at a science-fiction convention. I thought I might faint when she gave me a hug and we took a selfie together. 'Wow!' was the only word to describe the encounter, which left me breathless.

So, what is it about *Raiders of the Lost Ark* (and the Indiana Jones franchise in general) that has endured all these years and caused it to remain one of the most popular movies ever made?

I first saw *Raiders* on my own at a small cinema in St Ives, Cornwall, while I was on holiday with my family. My parents had been called away to attend the funeral of a family friend and my brother's girlfriend had come to keep him company. Not wanting to play gooseberry, I went to the cinema. I knew very little about the film going in and, in my naivety, actually thought it might be a film about that chap from the Bible called Noah. I had a seen a few stills and knew it was from the director of *Jaws* and the creator of *Star Wars*, but I didn't know much more than that.

As I took my seat and the lights went out, I was slowly introduced to an adventurer who was clearly following a treasure map in a dark jungle. Entering an ancient temple that no one has ever made it out of alive before, Indy survives a series of booby traps before managing to obtain the golden idol he has come for. After outrunning a giant boulder, he is captured by a rival who takes the prize from him. These two clearly have history! Having escaped, Indy races towards a river and a plane that will carry him out of there. But even then he's not totally out of the woods, as the pilot's pet snake is in the passenger seat. All obstacles dealt with, they fly off into the sunset.

End of film, right? I was absolutely exhausted by this point and genuinely got up out of my seat to leave, thinking, *Wow! That was fantastic.* But hang on… The film was still going.

And it just got better and better and better.

It got more exciting, more thrilling and scarier – and even in the midst of all that, it still managed to squeeze in the funniest moment ever committed to film (the bit where Indy deals with the giant sword-swinger). When my father saw it a year later, his laughter filled the whole cinema.

Raiders has everything: a touch of science fiction alongside moments of horror, romance, mystery and intrigue. The stunts are impressive and the story is remarkable.

It has some tremendous action sequences and great individual performances that make you believe in the characters and their predicaments. John Williams provides one of cinema's most majestic scores and Spielberg directs with a lightness of touch that makes the whole thing a joy. And who other than Harrison Ford could have breathed life into Indiana Jones? His knowing looks, boyish excitement and determination to see the job done keep us rooting for him every step of the way.

If the opening left me exhausted, the rest of the film

had me staggering out of the cinema in a daze of ecstasy. Cinematic perfection was, and is, the only accurate phrase for *Raiders of the Lost Ark*.

I've lost count of the number of times I have seen *Raiders* over the years. I know the script by heart and have owned it on pan and scan video, widescreen video, DVD and Blu-ray. I have several books on the making of the film and even saw it at the Royal Albert Hall a few years ago with a live orchestra providing the score. It was a truly wonderful evening.

The film also did something else for me. It sparked a lifelong fascination with the 'lost ark' (the Ark of the Covenant). Dr Brody (played by Denholm Elliott) misquotes the Bible at the start of the film. He says that the Bible guarantees victory to any army that has the ark, but the Bible is very clear that it was not a good-luck charm for anyone who possessed it. The ark was a sacred, powerful object that represented the presence of God. It was carried into battle, and when it was captured, Israel's enemies suffered the consequences.

Is the ark still around today, I wonder, waiting, as Belloq (Paul Freeman) suggests, in some antechamber yet to be discovered, or is it really in that monastery in Tibet? Did the Crusaders find it under the temple mount in Jerusalem, or did it end up in Babylon? Who knows? Is it, in fact, in heaven (John certainly sees it there in Revelation 11:19), or is that the original, and the one Moses made merely a copy? I just don't know.

I do know that now, thanks to Jesus Christ's sacrificial death on the cross, I don't need to bow before a gold box or enter a temple to meet with God. That's the old covenant –

Old Testament stuff. When Christ died, the curtain of the temple blocking us from God's presence was torn down, and now I can come directly into his presence. What a privilege that is. I need to make more of it – spending more time in prayer, more time reading the Bible and more time learning to listen to what God is saying to me.

Of course, just when we thought it was all over, Indy (and later Marion, played by Karen Allen) came back for one last adventure. *Indiana Jones and the Dial of Destiny* (2023) saw Ford ride out once again, seeking a device created by the famous Greek scholar Archimedes that could control time.

While *Dial of Destiny* had its critics, yours truly wasn't one of them. Not only was I grateful to have our great hero back, but the movie was also action-packed, witty and exciting, with another superb John Williams score. The concept of wanting to control time and change the course of history was nothing new, but it was well done in this film. The final shot indicates that maybe – just maybe – Indy's time isn't over yet… but we must wait and see. This acts as a reminder for me that our days are in God's hands, and thank goodness for that.

Speaking of Indy sequels and prequel (*Temple of Doom*, 1984), as good as those films are (or not… but even *Kingdom of the Crystal Skull* (2008) has its moments, and *The Last Crusade* (1989) is very good), none could ever match the breathtaking, exhausting, funny, scary, uplifting, amazing experience that is *Raiders of the Lost Ark*. It may be forty years old, but as Indy himself suggests, it's all about the mileage – and *Raiders* certainly goes the distance.

Intermission 7
Jesus Revolution (2023)

Director: Jon Erwin and Brent McCorkle
Starring: Jonathan Roumie, Joel Gurney, Kelsey Grammer

Yes, I know I'm a member of 'clergy corner' (a title Mark Kermode and Mayo on their podcast (*Kermode and Mayo's Take*) have bestowed on church ministers who review films), and so have a declared interest… but hear me out, please.

Jesus Revolution is worth seeing, regardless of your POV. It's a film about preachers that isn't preachy, but simply chooses to tell the story as it unfolded; a film based on well-documented historical events.

In 1968, Californian pastor Chuck Smith finds that his church is slowly dying and that he is unable to connect with the younger, free-living generation of hippies. After being introduced to a young, Bible-believing hippie called Lonnie Frisbee, things take a dramatic turn. Frisbee and his Jesus-loving friends transform Smith's church – a move that begins a movement.

It's not long before growing numbers mean that a new church is needed, and the word begins to spread – through California and beyond. The greatest charismatic, evangelical revival ever seen takes America by storm. This 'revival' was big news at the time, even making the cover of *Time* magazine. There were reports of supernatural healings and massive numbers of people being baptised.

This films offers a fascinating take on an unprecedented revival. Kelsey Grammer is superb as the initially bewildered Chuck Smith, and Jonathan Roumie (who plays Lonnie Frisbee) is as charismatic as his character. Less prominent characters are well fleshed out, and the film simply seeks to present the facts without asking us to judge them. What nobody can deny is that there was an amazing and incredible growth in the number of people becoming Christians during that period – especially young people.

Beautifully produced, shot and acted, the film portrays a unique moment in American history. Even if you are sceptical about such things, it will challenge you to reassess your point of view.

8
His name was Alfred Hitchcock

In 1946, an excellent psychological thriller called *The Spiral Staircase* was released. It was not a particularly big hit, but remains to this day an effective chiller. The film wasn't, but could have been, directed by Alfred Hitchcock (the actual director was Robert Siodmak, who made a string of B-movies through the 1940s and 50s).

The reason I bring this up is simple. I have a theory about Hitchcock's movies: he knew that stairs could be scary. You never know what's at the top, what's hiding at the bottom, and whether or not you're going to meet Norman Bates's mum halfway up.

The movies of Alfred Hitchcock have long been an obsession of mine, and I have often said that if I were ever to appear on *Mastermind* they would form my chosen specialist subject. He made fifty-three, and I own fifty-two of them.[3] So this chapter could be a long one, as there is a lot to say. I promise I will try to restrain myself.

Back to the subject of stairs. Scenes set on, or around, staircases are incredibly prevalent in Hitch's films, and are among some of the most important in his movies. I've already alluded to the fact that one character encounters Mrs Bates on the stairs in *Psycho* (1960). In *Frenzy* (1972), a murder takes place in an upper room in London, as the camera pans down a staircase and out onto a busy street. In *Strangers on a Train* (1951), a young girl is standing on a staircase listening to a conversation as she begins to figure out who the bad guy might be. In *Rebecca* (1940), Maxim de Winter experiences a fit of rage when he sees his new bride standing at the top of the stairs wearing a dress that belonged to his dead first wife, whose portrait hangs on the wall above her.

In *The Lodger: A Story of the London Fog* (1926, arguably the greatest silent movie ever made – told you I was biased), Hitchcock wanted to show characters in a downstairs room imagining what was happening upstairs. His brilliant solution was to use a glass ceiling. (By the way, this was also the first film in which Hitch made a cameo appearance, something that was to become a regular feature in his films.)

So, yes – stairs! There are more examples as well. Think of the end of *North by Northwest* (1959), where Cary Grant is upstairs in the baddie's house, watching Eva Marie

---

[3] Number fifty-three is a 1927 film called *The Mountain Eagle*. It's probably the most sought-after movie in the world, as it's long been lost and all we have left now are a few grainy black-and-white stills; tantalising clues as to what may well be another masterpiece. It will turn up one day… we hope!

Saint being held captive. Or how about the great scene in *Notorious*, where the camera pans down a grand, sweeping staircase and zooms in on a set of keys in our heroine's hands?

In *Rear Window* (1954) we watch with James Stewart as the suspected murderer returns home while Grace Kelly is searching his house. His climb up those stairs is agonisingly tense to watch. In *Vertigo* (1958), James Stewart (again) has to climb the steep, narrow steps of a large town in an effort to stop Kim Novak from committing suicide, but he suffers from vertigo and the question is, 'Will he get there in time?'

And then of course there's that famous walk up the stairs Tippi Hedren takes towards an attic room at the end of *The Birds* (1963). If you know the scene you will know just how terrifying it is – and yes, those were real birds that were flung at the petrified actress during that scene. It took five days to film, after which Tippi ended up having to go to hospital to be treated for trauma and exhaustion. She later claimed that Hitchcock put her through that torture as an act of revenge for her rejecting his advances. We won't get into that here. But for me it's one of the most terrifying scenes in cinematic history.

There are other examples, but you get the point. Stairs are scary, and Hitchcock, the master of suspense, knew it. They are the focus of many a great mystery.

For most people, the greatest mystery in life – the one that bothers, confuses and worries them most – is the ultimate one: what happens after death? Is there an afterlife? If so, do we go up or down? For those who believe there is something beyond the grave, the hope is that they will be going up – up to the great place, where 'the man upstairs' will welcome them in. Indeed, 'the man upstairs' has become such a common nickname for God that the concept of heaven being 'up' and hell being 'down' forms a complexly natural part of any conversation about what happens after we die.

As a Christian, I believe I am going up. I believe that Jesus will be waiting for me and that, because he has paid my 'entrance fee' to heaven, I will be welcomed in. But what if I'm wrong? What if there is no afterlife? What if everything I've said so far in this book isn't true at all?

If that's the case, then I've had a great life. I've met many wonderful people all over the world – well, Europe mostly – and have enjoyed countless social events at church, travelled, penned a book and written movie reviews for a best-selling magazine. If, at the end of it all, there's nothing more… well, fair enough, I gave it my best shot. But if I am right – if the *Bible's* right – and if the experiences I've had of God's presence, leading, guiding, provision and help are all real, then oh, boy, do I have something to look forward to.

As a full-time evangelist, I was once asked by someone without a faith if Christianity was nothing more than a life insurance policy. My reply was, 'No, it's an *eternal life* insurance policy.' Because of the death, resurrection, accession and felt presence of Jesus Christ, I know what's waiting for me when I 'go up'. I hope you do, too.

Stairs are scary. Hitchcock knew it, and his tremendous films are testament to that fact. But as for the great, final staircase we will all have to climb – it's not scary at all when you know who is waiting for you at the top!

Intermission 8
Typist Artist Pirate King (2022)

Director: Carol Morley
Starring: Monica Dolan, Kelly Macdonald, Gina McKee

As each year comes to an end, those of us who review movies are asked for our best and worst lists of the year's films. It's always a fun, but sometimes difficult, exercise. For me, 2022 proved exceptionally easy – and yet tricky at the same time. The reason for this was that I had two favourites and couldn't separate them in my affection. In joint first place were the science-fiction film *Lola* and a film called *Typist Artist Pirate King* (*TAPK* for short). If pushed, I probably would have gone for the latter – a poster of which, signed by the director and producer, now adorns my living room wall.

The writer of *TAPK* is a friend of mine. She is the UK's

leading film director Carol Morley, whose previous works include the sublime psychological detective thriller *Out of Blue* and the haunting mystery *The Falling*.

In *TAPK* she brings us something completely different. This is a fantasy biopic about the much-overlooked British artist, played by the brilliant Monica Doland. Audrey died in 2013, leaving behind thousands of pieces of art that had never been exhibited (as well as eighty scrapbooks containing everything from leaves to sweet wrappers). Audrey's time at the Royal Academy of Arts was short-lived, as she suffered from severe mental illness and spent much of her life in institutions. Her illness manifested itself in a very particular way. She would walk up to strangers and recognise them as people from her past.

Carol creates a scenario where, at the end of her life, Audrey persuades her psychiatric nurse Sandra – a wonderful performance by Kelly Macdonald – to drive her from London to Sunderland, where an art exhibition is taking place. Audrey sees this as her last opportunity to have her work displayed. Along the way they meet all sorts of characters from Audrey's past, and a mystery is resolved.

Carol also takes the opportunity to showcase the artist's work. In between key scenes, she fills the screen with Audrey's art, which is well worth seeing. This is a dark, funny, compelling, brilliantly scripted, and wonderfully acted and scored film – a must-see. I thoroughly recommend it, and not just because Carol is a friend.

9
Wishing upon a star

Time to get nostalgic… and show my age! Something I always enjoyed about bank holidays when I was growing up was sitting down and turning on the TV around teatime for *Disney Time*.

Younger readers may be shocked by this, but back in the day we had to wait not weeks, not months, but *years* to see films on TV after they were shown in cinemas. Today films can often be seen at home while they are still in the cinema, something that annoys me immensely, as it affects cinema takings and stops people from going.

Likewise, owning films on nice shiny discs or even on videotape was the stuff of science fiction. So, unless a film turned up on television you simply had no chance of seeing it. That's why the Christmas *Radio Times* was always a must-have. You would eagerly search the film listings and earmark the ones you had either missed at the cinema or wanted to see again. It was so thrilling. The Bond movie on ITV shown just after the Queen's Speech was usually shortened, but we simply didn't care. Bond was on!

Disney Time on a bank holiday was something we really looked forward to. A celebrity would introduce clips from some of the Disney classics, and you just lived in the hope that they would show a scene from your favourite film. You might get 'The Bare Necessities' (*The Jungle Book*, 1967), 'Little April Shower' (*Bambi*, 1942), a magical sword being pulled out of a rock (*The Sword in the Stone*, 1963), lots of black-and-white dogs running around (*One Hundred and One Dalmatians*, 1961), cats belting out jazz numbers (*The Aristocats*, 1970), wicked witches pronouncing curses (*Snow White*, 1937) and princes kissing beautiful princesses (*Sleeping Beauty*, 1959). The sense of anticipation was tangible.

Of course, many more Disney films have been released since that show ended back in the 1970s. If it was revived today, the choice of clips would be staggering. New methods of animation have arrived (did you know that *Beauty and the Beast* was the first animated film to feature a computer-generated scene?), new trends have been set and new ways of doing things have arrived. Disney is making films that reflect modern society with more diversity in the characters featured and social media making an appearance.

But it's the classics we remember. In addition to the ones mentioned above, we can add *The Little Mermaid* (1989), *Aladdin* (1992) and *The Lion King* (1994). These and others have wormed their way into our hearts, and most cinema fans couldn't imagine life without them.

However, perfect as these films are, it appears Disney felt

the need to either improve or reinvent them. As a result, we have seen most of the classics turned into live-action movies. The big question is, why? Why not just rerelease the classics and let us enjoy them in all their glory? Why attempt to breathe new life into something that wasn't dead in the first place?

The simple answer is: the almighty dollar. Money talks, and nowadays so do lions and beasts in live-action remakes. Few of these remakes have brought anything new to the table – the odd new song here and there – and the majority haven't been particularly successful at the box office.

That said, there are some exceptions. Will Smith did a terrific job of stepping into Robin Williams's shoes in the vibrant, funny, live-action version of *Aladdin* (2019). The ending of the new version of *The Jungle Book* (2016) was changed to bring it more in line with Rudyard Kipling's original story, and Halle Bailey did a wonderful job of capturing the essence of Ariel in the rather spectacular *Little Mermaid* (2023) remake. At the time of writing, I'm waiting to see how the forthcoming live version of *Snow White and the Seven Dwarfs* (due in 2025) will turn out.

In a very real sense, these films are a case of life imitating art. They are an attempt to bring new life to that which already exists. The fact that many have failed to improve on the originals – or even equal them – is testament to the fact that not everything new is necessarily good or worthwhile. Some things are best left alone, despite the odd exception.

Given all the suffering we see in the world today, it is not surprising that so many of us wish Disneyland was more than just a theme park. The animator promoted its first theme park as 'The Happiest Place On Earth': a place of joy, fun and escapism. I have only been to Disneyland once (the one in Florida), and it was nice to escape to a world of imagination and fantasy, where dreams come true. However, it reminded me of one simple fact: it's not real!

At the end of the day, you have to leave the park, go out into the massive car park and drive away. (Quick tip – if you do drive to Disney, make a careful note of which section of the car park you are in. It could save several hours of your life.) At some point, you have to re-enter the real world. A world where not every day is a Zip-a-Dee-Doo-Dah kind of day. Where bills have to be paid, people get old, and even a loving kiss can't bring someone back to life. Sadly, the world is not one big Disney theme park. Life does not always imitate art.

This is an interesting thought for me as a Christian because of something Jesus said. In John 10:10 (one of the easiest Bible references to remember), he said that he had come to earth so that we might 'have life, and have it to the full'. This is something many a Disney character – from Snow White and Beauty to Woody (OK, he's a Pixar character, but you get my drift) – have dreamed of. Imagine that! A life lived in all its fullness. Whoever you are, wherever you live, however young or old you are, and whether you are rich or poor – life in all its fullness.

What does that actually mean? No doubt everyone reading this will have a different answer. From owning a Ferrari (yes, please) to marrying the person of your dreams, to fulfilling your wildest ambitions, the options are endless. Bearing in mind these things may not actually happen, there has to be another meaning behind Jesus' words. For me, what he's getting at is simply this: I (Jesus) can offer a life that will bring you immense satisfaction because you will live the life God intended for you to live.

In my experience, and that of countless others living with and for Jesus, this doesn't mean you will get everything you want. But you will discover that he can provide everything you need. Trust him, believe in him, and the result will be a life of peace, joy and hope. After all, when Jesus said he came to offer us life, he meant the eternal variety.

It's simply a matter of trusting in him. If you already know the reality of this, the world you're living in should really give you something to sing about.

Intermission 9
Lola (2022)

Director: Andrew Legge
Starring: Emma Appleton, Stefanie Martini

During our last intermission, we took a look at my joint favourite film of 2022, Carol Morley's sublime *Typist Artist Pirate King*. It seems only fair to view the other one this time round. *Lola* was director Andrew Legge's directorial debut, and it's one of the most original and brilliantly shot films I have seen in a while. Sci-fi at its best.

The film is set in London in 1941. The city is under heavy bombardment from the Luftwaffe and things are very grim. However, in a hidden-away lab, two scientists – sisters – have created a machine they call Lola, which enables them to hear and see broadcasts from the future. The first thing they hear is 1970s pop music, and they fall in love with David Bowie. It's not long before they realise that having the ability to know what the future holds could seriously help the war effort. Knowing when and where the Germans were going to attack meant British forces could get there first and see them off. Unfortunately, things quickly start to go wrong. Changing the future has consequences… terrible ones.

This film is shot in black-and-white and projected in a square format. The idea is that we are watching events as they unfolded in 1941 using 1941 technology. The special photographic effects are tremendous (reminiscent of the way Forrest Gump was placed alongside historical figures). Suffice it to say that I absolutely loved this film and highly recommend it to you. See it as soon as you can!

I recently met the director, who says he is already working on his next sci-fi film. I can't wait.

10
But how did it all begin?

It's a widely held misconception that the very first silent film was shown by the Lumière Brothers in France. The film was imaginatively entitled *L'arrivée d'un Train en Gare de La Ciotat* (*Arrival of a Train at La Ciotat*, 1896) and depicted just that: a train arriving at the station in La Ciotat on the French Mediterranean coast. When the film was first screened, it is claimed that audiences ran screaming from the theatre, believing that the train was about to crash through the screen and land right on top of them. There is probably some truth to this, though some believe the story was made up to encourage thrill-seekers to go and see the movie.

However, this certainly wasn't the first time a moving image had been shown on screen. In fact, let's just do a quick rundown of cinematic firsts. The first film, as far we can tell, was entitled *Roundhay Garden Scene* (1888). Filmed in Roundhay, Leeds, the footage depicts French director Louis Le Prince's son, Adolphe, his in-laws the Whitleys, and a woman named Annie Hartley enjoying an afternoon in the garden of Oakwood Grange, the Whitleys' home. This is the oldest surviving moving footage we have.

The first commercial screening of a film was – here we go again – run by the Lumière Brothers. Screened on 28 December 1895 at the Grande Café in Paris, *La Sortie des Ouvriers de l'Usine Lumière* (*Workers Leaving the Lumière Factory*) was a very simple film that showed scenes of everyday life in and around Paris.

The first feature-length silent movie released in 1906, was a Western: *The Story of the Kelly Gang*. Full of action, the film was just over an hour long and was the longest-running film the world had ever seen at that time. The rest, as they say, is history.

Confession time... For someone who considers himself a bit of a movie nut (you may have got that impression), I have never been a big fan of silent comedies or comedians. I appreciate the genius of Charlie Chaplin, Buster Keaton, and Laurel and Hardy. They were absolute geniuses, of course. Their comic timing, sense of location and bravery are unparalleled. But I do find – particularly with Chaplin's early work – the stories a little repetitive. It's not until the end of his career, when he starts tackling big subjects such as the Second World War and the machination of society that his work becomes really interesting.

Keaton was more daring in his films. Doing his own stunts and literally risking death, his work is much more interesting to me – although he still had some way to go to beat Harold Lloyd. Who could forget Lloyd hanging from the hands of a clock above a busy street in *Safety Last!* (1923) That title says a lot about the era.

But silent films are not just about the great comics who put their talent up on a big screen for all to see. Every genre you can think of was tackled by those early pioneers of cinema. You name it, they made it. Alongside Westerns and comedies, there were also sci-fi films, thrillers, romcoms, fantasy adventures and biblical epics.

Long before Judy Garland made it to Oz in 1939, the tale had already been told. There had been three versions of Oz, including a 1925 film in which Oliver Hardy played the Tin Man. Other books that were to be turned into movies included the first version of *Ben-Hur* (1925) to be filmed, *The Birth of a Nation* (1915), *The Mask of Zorro* (1920) and *Faust* (1926).

Even at this early stage, Hollywood was starting to notice the potential of bringing history to life on the big screen, and some really went to town. Abel Gance's *Napoléon* remains one of the greatest (and longest) historical dramas ever. Filmed in 1927, the film, which has been restored in recent years, is more than five hours long. It was probably the first film to have an intermission.

Another epic, and one of my favourite films of all time, came to us from Germany. In fact, Germany was very influential in the development of cinema. German Expressionism suddenly became a thing. With its use of dark lighting, sober tones, massive sets and often difficult – even horrific – stories, it changed the face of cinema and is still having an impact today. Hitchcock went to Germany to learn all about it.

The film I am referring to comes from one of cinema's

other great directors, Fritz Lang. His film *Metropolis* (1927) is a classic work of science fiction. It tells the story of a great city where the rich enjoy every luxury under the sun while the lower classes toil away, operating huge machines far below the city and living in poverty. Eventually, a heroine in the form a robot girl, Maria, arrives and becomes a long-awaited messiah (she was also the inspiration for C-3PO in *Star Wars*).

Metropolis was a flop at first, and it is only in retrospect that it has come to be seen for the classic that it is. You may recall that Queen used scenes from the film in their video for the hit single 'Radio Ga Ga'. If you have never seen it, it's a must-watch. So, by the way, is *Journey to the Moon* (1902), another famous image of a spaceship that crashes into the eye of the man in the moon. It's a very weird film, but great fun.

A chapter on silent movies could go on forever, and I have no intention of doing that. However, I do want to point out that there was another trend in those early years that is worth noting.

As I have mentioned before, there was another source of material for early film-makers: the Bible. Both the Old and New Testaments provided stories deemed worthy of filming. There was *The Life and Passion of Jesus Christ* (1903), *Samson and Deliah* (1922) and *Noah's Ark* (1928), all of which are worth seeing.

One of my great frustrations as a film fan is trying to persuade younger people to watch older films. Films in – shock horror – black and white! Films that have no dialogue. Films made without the aid of computers. I love these silent movies and have mentioned some of my favourites here. Without those early, bold pioneers we might never have had cinema as we know and love it today. We owe them a debt we can never repay. It's where it all began.

It kind of reminds me of those early missionaries who first took the story of Jesus around the world. Where would we be without them? The gospel is the greatest story ever told, as we see in *The Birth, the Life and the Death of Jesus Christ* (1906). Without the gospel story, we would be nowhere.

Intermission 10
Mrs Harris Goes to Paris (2022)

Director: Antony Fabian
Starring: Lesley Manville, Isabelle Huppert, Lambert Wilson

I must confess that I went into this film thinking it really wasn't going to be my thing. A film about a cleaning woman buying a dress. Come on…. But how wrong can a person be?

You know when you see movie posters that say 'Charming', 'A joy', 'A real treat', 'A delight' – well this film was all of that and more. It really is a lovely, uplifting and joyful film that sends you out of the cinema with a spring in your step.

This is the third time the 1958 novel has been filmed. The previous version was made in 1992, with Angela Lansbury in the title role – only she was known as Mrs 'Arris. In the 2022 edition, Lesley Manville brings the character to life and does so wonderfully. She hardly stops smiling as the working-class cleaner who harbours a dream of buying a Christian Dior dress. She saves up and gets herself to Paris… and all sorts of fun ensues. I won't say much more, but expect romance, misunderstandings, the formation of unusual friendships, and an important message about class and social structure.

One of the greatest aspects of the film is that it has a strong message, but it certainly isn't preachy. The message relates to the unfair way in which society treats those it regards as being of an inferior class. Mrs Harris shows that, with a bit of determination, dedication and faith, our dreams can come true. The Parisian scenes, set during a refuse collectors' strike, remind us just how much we rely on the Mrs Harrises of the world, and that everyone should be treated with equal respect, regardless of their wealth and social status. All of that comes across clearly, and yet the film remains incredibly entertaining and a total joy.

This movie didn't quite pan out the way I'd expected, yet in a way it did. That will make more sense when you see it. But I have to say that because of the performances, the score and the settings – yes, even the dresses – this film really captured my heart, and I thoroughly enjoyed it from start to finish.

11
Woya woya way, woo woo wa!

OK, I'll admit it… that's not very good. It's supposed to be a verbal representation of the famous opening chords from arguably the greatest Western ever made. Ennio Morricone's iconic score for *The Good, the Bad and the Ugly* (1966) is one of the most recognisable pieces of film music ever written. So good, in fact, that when Hugo Montenegro recorded it as a single, he had a number-one hit with it in 1968.

The film is about three men looking for lost treasure and eventually finding it in a deserted graveyard. Set against the backdrop of the civil war, it is brutal and violent, yet also emotionally draining. The final stand-off scene is enhanced by the fact that the director, Sergio Leone, brought loudspeakers to the set and had the music playing as the action took place. It's an incredible piece of cinema, and without a doubt my favourite Western.

Which actually is interesting. Mention Westerns to most people and they will immediately start talking about 'cowboys and Indians'. The image of John Wayne mounting his horse and going after wild savages who have captured his girl springs to mind. You might have pictured wagons being drawn around in circles and cowboys cooking beans when the Indians come charging in, only for the calvary to come riding to the rescue. That's a Western – and there are many, many films that fit this criteria.

But look a bit closer, and you'll see that Westerns are so much more than that. The stories they tell are many and varied, not just your stereotypical good guys versus bad guys. They tell stories about treasure hunters, but they also tell stories about love and injustice. They tell stories about gang rivalry and racism. They tell stories about unlikely heroes and cultural challenges. They tell stories about the environment and the wider world. They are a right mixed bunch, and that what's makes them so interesting.

One of the first feature-length movies was a Western called *The Story of the Kelly Gang* (1906), and they have been a staple of cinema ever since. Partly because of where Hollywood was located and partly because they appealed to the American sense of nationalism and pride, Westerns were quickly and easily rolled out, producing some of Hollywood's biggest stars – including John Wayne, Henry Fonda and Gary Cooper – along the way.

Let's just pause for a moment and take a look at some of the films that tend to veer away from what we might think of as typical Westerns, while maintaining the same distinctive feel. Films we need to note include the following. (If your favourite isn't listed here, I can only apologise.)

The Big Country (1958)
An epic directed by a man used to directing epics. William Wyler would go on to make *Ben-Hur* the following year. The film follows the adventures of a former sea captain who is heading out west to visit his fiancée, who lives on a large ranch. The plot involves local gang rivalry and has plenty of action. It was a massive hit and the second most successful film in the UK in 1959. Like most Westerns, it featured a terrific score by Jerome Moross and stands up to repeated viewings.

How the West Was Won (1962)
Another epic put together by three directors and divided up into five chapters. The film follows a group of pioneers as they move out to explore and conquer Western America. Once again, the civil war has a large part to play in the plot. At 164 minutes, the film does require a bit of patience at times, but the set pieces are worth waiting for.

The Magnificent Seven (1960)
And again, everyone knows the music. I bet you're humming it now. Elmer Bernstein beautifully captures the spirit, adventure and, above all else, the hope of those who live in a poor village and are being terrorised by local bandits. Rounding up the seven gun-shooters of the day and offering to pay them whatever they wanted, this film is undoubtedly one of the greatest ever made. The all-star cast includes Steve McQueen, Yul Brynner and Charles Bronson. So successful was this film that it spawned three sequels.

High Noon (1952)
Filmed in real time, Gary Cooper is a marshal determined to stand alone against a gang of bandits, despite the pleadings of the townsfolk and his fiancée. What ensues is chilling, tense, nail-biting stuff. Again, the music is outstanding. The great Dimitri Tiomkin provided a score that gave nothing away and Tex Ritter's version of 'Do Not Forsake Me, O My Darling' ('The Ballad of High Noon') was a bit hit. This one is a must-see.

Gunfight at the O.K. Corral (1957)
Wyatt Earp and Doc Holliday go up against Billy Clanton's gang in a film based on an actual event. The actual gunfight happened on 26 October 1881 and – get this – lasted less than a minute. But that didn't stop director John Sturges from making a fantastic film out of the story and casting two Hollywood legends in the form of Burt Lancaster and Kirk Douglas.

Blazing Saddles (1974)
A comedy Western that deals with racism and features one of the funniest scenes involving beans in cinema history. Mel Brooks's outrageous satire is funny but telling. Relating the story of the appointment of a black (shock horror!) sheriff who attempts to bring law and order to a rundown town, this film was a box office smash.

Dances With Wolves (1990)
Another film with – guess what – a stunning score (this time by John Barry). Kevin Costner plays Lieutenant John Dunbar, who is assigned to a remote civil war outpost and

finds himself building a relationship with a nearby Sioux settlement, causing him to ask questions about his own beliefs and standards. Beautifully shot, the film captivates audiences from the very first frame.

And of course, we could go on. But the aim of the exercise here is to graphically illustrate that not all Westerns are about cowboys and Indians. These films deal with a wide variety of themes and take a fascinating look at the human condition. They examine how people can survive in the most desperate, poverty-stricken circumstances and are testament to the human spirit to survive.

There is of course a lot of religion in these films. Every town, outpost and army base has a chapel. There is always a chaplain on hand to give advice, and of course you will hear many old hymns, most notably 'Shall We Gather at the River?'. God is present even in the old and very wild West, and he is needed. The Good Book ultimately lays down the law even in the most lawless of societies. People gather for worship and draw strength in doing so. It seems as if there is no escape from God wherever you go.

Psalms 139:8-10 says: 'If I go up to the heavens, you are there; if I make my bed in the depths, you are there. If I rise on the wings of the dawn, if I settle on the far side of the sea, even there your hand will guide me, your right hand will hold me fast.' This is a point that makers of Western films seem genuinely happy to uphold.

Intermission 11
Avatar: The Way of Water (2022)

Director: James Cameron
Starring: Sam Worthington, Zoe Saldana, Sigourney Weaver

Sequels… love them or loathe them, they are an inevitable fact of life for us film fans. They can offer a joyous reunion with much-loved characters or a sad letdown if they are not quite as great or charismatic the second (or tenth) time around. As a film critic, I am often asked about sequels. Among my own personal favourites I would have to list the following: *Star Trek II: The Wrath of Khan* (1982), *Superman II* (1980), *The Godfather Part II* (1974), *The Empire Strikes Back* (1980) and *Toy Story 2* (1999), *3* (2010) and, well, let's include *4* (2019) in there as well.

Two significant sequels arrived in 2022: *Top Gun: Maverick* and *Avatar: The Way of Water*. We had to wait thirty-six years for a sequel to Tom Cruise's hit film *Top Gun* (1986), but boy was it worth it. The film just blew us all away and was a massive hit, proving, if proof be needed, that sequels can be as good as, if not better than, the original. It's a superb film and a worthy companion of the original.

Then we have *Avatar: The Way of Water*. James Cameron's recording-breaking first instalment (the highest-grossing movie in history) came out in December 2009 and, unlike *Top Gun*, nobody was really screaming for sequel. But the fact that one appeared after a thirteen-year wait surprised no one. Apparently, it's the first of five that are planned. And just in case we had really been missing the planet Pandora, James Cameron decided that the sequel should be long. Very long. More than three hours long! I felt every one of those minutes.

Let's be honest, *Avatar: The Way of Water* is dull, boring, ponderous, pointless, and a waste of time and money. A lot of money. It's just not very good. Yes, it looks great – I saw it on a big, big screen in 3D and it looked wonderful. But as we all know, looks aren't everything. The reason why the sequels I mentioned above work is because the stories they tell are so good. This film has such a weak storyline that I gave up caring about an hour in. Actually, it may have been less than that. I know I was awake – but only just.

Cameron is so in love with the world he created that he neglected a fundamental principle of storytelling: tell a story! It's fine to immerse us the environment of an alien planet, but for that to become more important than the story is, frankly, unforgiveable. What is even worse is that when the semblance of a story does begin to surface above the waters of Pandora, it is so clichéd you can immediately guess what is coming. What is it with Cameron and sinking ships, anyway?

So… sequels. Some are magnificent and even better than the original, but some are not. This one definitely isn't.

12
Burning bridges

Sadly, more than 110 armed conflicts are taking place around the world as I type this. From Ukraine to the Middle East, nation is fighting nation, tribe is fighting tribe, and humans are inflicting untold horrors on their fellow humans in the name of freedom and liberty… but mostly, in reality, to gain power.

It will be interesting to see how many, if any, of the current conflicts are later turned into movies. After all, most wars have been. From the Zulu wars of the 1870s to Vietnam, war has provided cinema with enough material to produce hundreds of films. The question is: should we be entertained by these, bearing in mind the horrors they display? The fact of the matter is, we are, and some of the greatest movies ever made are war movies.

Spielberg's *Saving Private Ryan* (1998) is one that instantly springs to people's minds. Its graphic and shocking portrayal of the D-Day landings remains an outstanding landmark in cinematic history. Frankly, it's horrific. We see severed limbs, sand blowing up right in our faces, soldiers clearly terrified by what they are facing, and blood everywhere. The film, which won five Oscars, is a modern-day classic. It graphically illustrates the dilemma cinemagoers face: are we meant to enjoy this or are we being educated about the reality of what happened?

The same question applies when it comes to films about the Holocaust. *The Zone of Interest* (2023) offered an intense, emotionally draining focus on the Höss family living a normal domestic life with Auschwitz just the other side of the garden fence. I didn't enjoy it at all, but I thought it was a fantastic film. The same goes for *Son of Saul* (2015) and *The Boy in the Striped Pyjamas* (2008). I felt educated but not necessarily entertained, which suggests that these films are necessary.

Other war movies that I have not enjoyed but really appreciated because of what they have taught me about war, why it happens, and its dreadful consequences, include *The Killing Fields* (1994); *Mash* (1970); *All Quiet on the Western Front* (1930 and 2022); and *Apocalypse Now* (1979). These are all powerful films, and films that should be seen. Several have won many awards, and rightly so. But are they entertaining?

War films tend to be at their most entertaining, for us Brits at any rate, when they show the UK at its finest and most heroic. We warm to these because they remind us that, at the end of the day, we won the war. This explains why films like *The Great Escape* (1963), *The Colditz Story* (1955), *The Dam Busters* (1955) and *Battle of Britain* (1969) are so popular. These films are not only well made, and populated by a host of stars, but they tell true stories of heroes who deserve all the praise that comes their way. These are entertaining war films because we can watch them secure in the knowledge that our heroes' actions are justified and enabled us to defeat evil. We can watch them knowing that all will be well. I fully expect Christopher Nolan's epic film *Dunkirk* (2017) and Joe Wright's *Darkest Hour* (2017) to join them in the pantheon of classics. Gary Oldman's performance as Churchill in the latter film is staggering.

But there's something else. These films act as a warning to those who might attempt to challenge us again. They convey the strong sentiment that we won't give up, we won't give in and we won't be defeated. They give us confidence about our future. We Brits will never, ever be captured and oppressed. And given the state of the world at the moment, that's important. Our place in the world is as it is because of our history, and Brits tend to assume this is an indication that God is on our side… so woe betide anyone who comes against us!

There is one other film I haven't mentioned yet that ranks very highly in my list of top war films. Released in 1970 with an all-star cast including Telly Savalas and Clint Eastwood, *Kelly's Heroes* is a very different sort of war movie. A disgruntled band of American GIs learn about a hold of gold held in a bank in a town behind enemy lines, and go after it. The film is very funny, has some genuinely tense moments and still manages to display the horrors of war as several members of the gang we get to know meet their untimely ends.

The theme of the film is ultimately about individuals

taking care of themselves, and to hell with the war going on around them. These soldiers see a chance to grab a fortune, and therefore a future for themselves, when all hope seems lost. The film was a big hit, and deservedly so. But it's that central theme that makes it stand out as a war film: the individual against the world. Actually, it turns out that in creating a pathway through to the bank they actually help their own army make it through the enemy lines as well. So everybody wins.

Something else I love about the film is the music, which is by Lalo Schifrin. Schifrin is a prolific composer who has written music for many great films, including a number of Clint Eastwood movies. The film is bookended by a great song that is heard over the opening and end titles. It took me quite a while to find the soundtrack on vinyl, and shortly after I did it came out on CD. Never mind. Performed by the Mike Curb Congregation, the song is called 'Burning Bridges'. It describes the life of a man who keeps seeing opportunities come his way and missing them. He has so many chances to move forward but keeps burning the bridges that would have led to a better future. It's an upbeat song with a downbeat theme. In the context of film, it seems to be saying, 'Don't miss any chances to change your life for the better', as those chances don't come along too often – and it makes sense.

Every time I hear it, it reminds me that I only have one life – so I had better make the most of it. As we've already discussed, Jesus said that he came so that we could live a full life (John 10:10). In other words, when I allow Jesus and his way and teachings to dictate the way I live my life, I am going to find the satisfaction I have been looking for. Having Jesus as my friend, my Lord and the one who shows me how to live makes life worth living. I have burned a few bridges in my life, but the one that led me to Jesus was the only one truly worth walking across.

War movies have always been with us and always will be. In the years to come, we may well see movies based on conflicts that are taking place today. They are not always an easy watch. They can challenge us, horrify us and make us sick to the pits of our stomachs about people's inhumanity towards one another. They can shock us and move us to the very core of our being. But they can also entertain us. They can remind us that we are (or were) on the winning side. They can inspire us as we watch our heroes conquering in the face of overwhelming odds. They can spur us on to want to do great deeds. But above all, they can encourage us to ask ourselves: what would we do and how far would we go to protect our loved ones and stand up for our values? Which bridges would we be willing to burn?

These questions are worth asking. For many years my parents had a plaque on their front room wall that had embedded on it a quote from the book of Joshua. It simply said: 'As for me and my household, we will serve the Lord' (Joshua 24:15). Joshua was a man who knew what it was to fight many wars. He made sure he was on the right side – the Lord's side. I hope everyone reading this is on the Lord's side as well.

Intermission 12
Desperation Road (2023)

Director: Nadine Crocker
Starring: Willa Fitzgerald, Ryan Hurst

This new film from director Nadine Crocker (who also directed *Cabin Fever*) is a hard-hitting drama that holds the attention from the start. Willa Fitzgerald plays Maben, a single mother, who is heading back to the small town she came from when she is raped by a bent cop in a motel carpark. However, when he turns his back on her, she manages to grab her gun and shoot him.

At the same time, Larry (Ryan Hurst) is heading home to the same small town, having just been released from prison. As the story unfolds, the two meet up and a relationship begins to develop. Sharing her secret with Larry, Maben begins to depend on him for protection.

Mel Gibson plays Larry's father in the kind of role we are getting used to seeing him in these days: the wise, all-knowing old guy who is happy to dispense advice.

This is a good, tight drama with an overriding theme of revenge and a good score by Haim Mazar. It's certainly worth a watch.

100 of the best

From magazines to film institutions, from movie clubs to TV shows and podcasts, everybody does it. Sooner or later, every film critic ends up producing their own 'top 100 movies of all time' list. Very often there is a great deal of similarity in those lists, with critics generally agreeing on the most worthy, artistic and serious films ever made. Far too often, however, those lists fail to include the more commercially successful films that audiences love.

So here is my list, submitted for your reading pleasure. Many of the films mentioned here have of course been referred to in this book. As you go down it and maybe tick off the ones you have seen – or even better the ones you haven't seen but would like to – take a moment to reflect on what those films have to say about faith, the human condition and your own situation. Or if you prefer, just enjoy the list and revel in the memory of some great movies.

Here we go… one thing I can guarantee is that this list will be different from any other you have seen. Feel free to disagree – that's what it's all about.

- ☐ 1. *Raiders of the Lost Ark* (1981)
- ☐ 2. *Close Encounters of the Third Kind* (1977)
- ☐ 3. *Alien* (1979)
- ☐ 4. *La La Land* (2016)
- ☐ 5. *Psycho* (1960)
- ☐ 6. *Planet of the Apes* (1968)
- ☐ 7. *On Her Majesty's Secret Service* (1969)
- ☐ 8. *An American Werewolf in London* (1981)
- ☐ 9. *Last Night in Soho* (2021)
- ☐ 10. *The Wizard of Oz* (1939)
- ☐ 11. *Die Hard* (1988)
- ☐ 12. *Back to the Future* (1985)
- ☐ 13. *Back to the Future Part II* (1989)
- ☐ 14. *Back to the Future Part III* (1990)
- ☐ 15. *The Lord of the Rings: The Return of the King* (2003)
- ☐ 16. *The Lord of the Rings: The Fellowship of the Ring* (2001)
- ☐ 17. *The Lord of the Ring: The Two Towers* (2002)
- ☐ 18. *No Time to Die* (2021)
- ☐ 19. *Vertigo* (1958)
- ☐ 20. *Rear Window* (1954)
- ☐ 21. *Strangers on a Train* (1951)
- ☐ 22. *Typist Artist Pirate King* (2022)
- ☐ 23. *Toy Story* (1995)
- ☐ 24. *Toy Story 2* (1999)
- ☐ 25. *Speed* (1994)
- ☐ 26. *Star Trek II: The Wrath of Khan* (1982)
- ☐ 27. *The Great Escape* (1963)
- ☐ 28. *The Good, the Bad and the Ugly* (1966)
- ☐ 29. *Twelve Angry Men* (1957)
- ☐ 30. *My Fair Lady* (1964)
- ☐ 31. *The Jungle Book* (1967)

- ☐ 32. *Casablanca* (1942)
- ☐ 33. *Metropolis* (1927)
- ☐ 34. *The Lodger* (1927)
- ☐ 35. *Village of the Damned* (1960)
- ☐ 36. *The Incredible Shrinking Man* (1957)
- ☐ 37. *Singin' in the Rain* (1952)
- ☐ 38. *Blade Runner* (1982)
- ☐ 39. *Indiana Jones and the Last Crusade* (1989)
- ☐ 40. *2001: A Space Odyssey* (1968)
- ☐ 41. *The Shawshank Redemption* (1994)
- ☐ 42. *Jaws* (1975)
- ☐ 43. *Aliens* (1986)
- ☐ 44. *The Muppet Christmas Carol* (1992)
- ☐ 45. *Casino Royale* (2006)
- ☐ 46. *Shaun of the Dead* (2004)
- ☐ 47. *Sunset Boulevard* (1950)
- ☐ 48. *Double Indemnity* (1944)
- ☐ 49. *Yesterday* (2019)
- ☐ 50. *Rocketman* (2019)
- ☐ 51. *Some Like It Hot* (1959)
- ☐ 52. *The Omen* (1976)
- ☐ 53. *From Russia with Love* (1963)
- ☐ 54. *Airplane!* (1980)
- ☐ 55. *Star Trek VI: The Undiscovered Country* (1991)
- ☐ 56. *Silent Running* (1972)
- ☐ 57. *Beauty and the Beast* (1991)
- ☐ 58. *Mary Poppins Returns* (2018)
- ☐ 59. *The Thing* (1982)
- ☐ 60. *South Pacific* (1958)
- ☐ 61. *The Holdovers* (2023)
- ☐ 62. *When Marnie Was There* (2014)

- ☐ 63. *King Kong* (1933)
- ☐ 64. *War of the Worlds* (1953)
- ☐ 65. *Bambi* (1942)
- ☐ 66. *Ghostbusters* (1984)
- ☐ 67. *High Society* (1956)
- ☐ 68. *Carry on Screaming!* (1966)
- ☐ 69. *The Birds* (1963)
- ☐ 70. *Jurassic Park* (1993)
- ☐ 71. *The Silence of the Lambs* (1991)
- ☐ 72. *Get out* (2017)
- ☐ 73. *For a Few Dollars More* (1965)
- ☐ 74. *Pulp Fiction* (1994)
- ☐ 75. *The Usual Suspects* (1995)
- ☐ 76. *The Seventh Seal* (1957)
- ☐ 77. *Grease* (1978)
- ☐ 78. *The Dark Knight* (2008)
- ☐ 79. *The Truman Show* (1998)
- ☐ 80. *Dr Strangelove or: How I Stopped Worrying and Learned to Love the Bomb* (1964)
- ☐ 81. *All the President's Men* (1976)
- ☐ 82. *The Purple Rose of Cairo* (1985)
- ☐ 83. *Seven* (1995)
- ☐ 84. *Monty Python and the Holy Grail* (1975)
- ☐ 85. *The Cabinet of Dr. Caligari* (1920)
- ☐ 86. *Don't Look Now* (1973)
- ☐ 87. *The Exorcist* (1973)
- ☐ 88. *Bonnie and Clyde* (1967)
- ☐ 89. *Toy Story 4* (2019)
- ☐ 90. *Indiana Jones and the Dial of Destiny* (2023)
- ☐ 91. *Goldfinger* (1964)
- ☐ 92. *The Shining* (1980)

- ☐ 93. *Dunkirk* (2017)
- ☐ 94. *Wild Rose* (2018)
- ☐ 95. *All Quiet on the Western Front* (1930)
- ☐ 96. *M* (1931)
- ☐ 97. *Lola* (2022)
- ☐ 98. *The Great Dictator* (1940)
- ☐ 99. *Paint Your Wagon* (1969)
- ☐ 100. *Frequently Asked Questions About Time Travel* (2009 – you probably won't find this one on similar lists, but check it out. It's terrific!)

Conclusion

I began this book by telling you about my first ever, life-changing, trip to the cinema to see *The Wizard of Oz*. Since that momentous day, I have lost count of the number of films I have seen at the cinema and at home. I don't have a clue, but it must be in the thousands.

My overriding point is that the movies have taught me so many lessons about life and faith, that when I stop to think about it there are just too many to list. Many have taught me about the value of human life and the importance of integrity and honesty. They have shown me right from wrong. They have helped me to learn lessons from history and consider where we are going as a human race. They have comforted me, challenged me, and made me laugh and cry.

But let's be honest. Above and beyond everything else, they've entertained me. They have just given me – well, most of them – a very, very good time, and for a couple of hours helped me to escape from the real world, to forget about all my problems. For me, there is nothing like going to the cinema and getting lost in another world, facing someone else's dilemmas – laughing, fighting, hoping, gasping and standing with characters who are as far removed from my world as I am from theirs. There is nothing better.

But if the movies weren't there, if you were to give me the devastating news that I could never see another one again, it would be OK, because – even more than films – one thing above all others has been consistent in my life and provided me with everything I need. That is, my faith in God and his son, Jesus Christ. Jesus is not a fictional character who once did something amazing, but a living, risen Saviour who helps me to live in the real world – from which I escape now and then by going to the cinema. That's what really makes life worth living. And the greatest thing of all about the Lord Jesus is that he'll be back one day.

Epilogue: More favourite reviews

End-of-credits scenes
A lot of movies these days have scenes at the end of the credits. Often they are not worth the wait, but I hope that what follows below will be. Here are a few more of my favourite reviews, some interviews I have had the privilege of conducting, and some thoughts on films to use for a men's night at your church or organisation. Enjoy. The credits will be rolling soon, I promise!

Rock Hudson: All That Heaven Allows (2023)

Director: Stephen Kijak
Starring: Rock Hudson, Roy Scherer, Ken Hodge

Ask any film fan, 'Who is your favourite actor?', and it won't be long before Rock Hudson's name crops up in the conversation. With a career that spanned three decades and more than thirty films, Hudson established himself as one of the Hollywood elite while harbouring a secret that caused him great pain and distress, and ultimately led to his death.

This documentary goes into great depth about that secret, as well as giving many revealing glimpses into his acting, relationships and private life. And that secret? Hudson was gay and had contracted AIDS. In fact, he was the first major celebrity to die from that awful disease on 2 October 1985, aged fifty-nine.

This is an excellent, compelling and gripping documentary that deserves to be widely seen. There are contributions from family members, fellow actors and friends who knew him well. The various film clips featured in the documentary showcase the variety of his work and give us an overview of how he got to where he was, as one of the greats of Hollywood.

I would recommend it to anyone interested in the history of cinema and the long-term treatment of gay people. It's also a reminder of how AIDS was treated in the 1980s when it first emerged.

An excellent watch.

Corsage (2022)

Director: Marie Kreutzer
Starring: Vicky Krieps, Florian Teichtmeister

I headlined my review of this film for *Sorted* by saying

that it was a delightful period drama with a terrific central performance. Funny, witty and moving, this biopic covers a year in the life of Elizabeth, Empress of Austria. On Christmas Eve 1877, Elizabeth – famed for her beauty, grace and charm – turns forty and enters a whole new era of existence. Deemed an old lady, she rallies against this label by engaging in a series of love affairs while travelling, as well as undergoing an extreme weight-loss regime and acting against type in 'proper' society.

Although mostly made up, this is a terrifically engaging biopic that keeps the audience captivated through a clever script and great performances. Vicky Krieps is fantastic in the lead role and dominates the screen. She has a charismatic presence and is wonderfully entertaining. She has an excellent supporting cast behind her and a director who seems content to just let her go and live the part. There is a freedom to her performance and a lightness that just seems to shout that she was left to her own devices.

The film has a great score and makes excellent use of modern songs. Who knew that Kris Kristofferson was popular in the late nineteenth century? It's actually all part of the fun. And it should be noted that there are some genuine laughs in this film.

Corsage deserves to be a big hit. Its excellent performances, creative costumes, beautiful scenery and varied music all make for a wonderfully entertaining film that should attract a wide audience.

Downton Abbey: A New Era (2022)

Director: Simon Curtis
Starring: Hugh Bonneville, Jim Carter, Michelle Dockery

I hope you will forgive me, but I don't want to go into too much detail about the plot of this wonderful, delightful, funny, engaging and, in the end, moving film. The less you know going in, the better.

I confess that I have never seen the TV series, so my only knowledge of *Downton* had been gleaned from seeing the first film (*Downton Abbey*, 2019), which I really enjoyed. However, that did not spoil my enjoyment of the sequel, *Downton Abbey: A New Era*, which is a superb piece of cinematic entertainment.

I laughed, I cried and I sighed with contentment. I honestly couldn't think of a bad thing to say about this film if I tried. Everything from the acting to the direction to the script is pitch perfect. It should have won prizes for performances, sets and costumes at the very least. Fans of the series will, I think, be more than satisfied, while the rest of us will just have a very good time.

There are two plots going on here in tandem. One involves an inherited villa in the south of France, which raises questions about Lord Grantham's heritage. The other concerns Downton itself being turned into a film set. Suffice it to say that 'Downton does Singin' in the Rain' sums it up well.

True, there are no shootouts or superheroes battling evil demons. There's no search for lost treasure and nothing blows up or gets attacked by aliens – all the stuff I usually love in a film. But watching this, I didn't care. I was just having a very good time. It offered a welcome change of pace and was well worth my time.

Downton Abbey: A New Era is enormously fun and totally captivating, and was well worth seeing on the big screen with its beautiful scenery. This was one of my favourite films of 2022, and believe me, no one – and I mean *no one* – is more surprised to be typing those words than I am. Go and see it! Lose yourself in a bygone era and have fun as you watch the start of a new one.

Father Stu (2022)

Director: Rosalind Ross
Starring: Mark Wahlberg, Mel Gibson, Jacki Weaver

This is a remarkable film that tells a remarkable story. It is the true story of an ex-boxer, alcoholic and would-be actor who ended up becoming a priest and firm believer in God, despite facing what proved to be a terminal battle with a muscle-wasting disease. Mark Wahlberg is excellent as the cynical sceptic who turns believer. He is ably supported by an excellent cast, including fellow believer (in real life) and committed Catholic Mel Gibson, who plays his father.

Stuart Long (Wahlberg) goes to Hollywood to make his fortune, but instead he meets Carmen (Teresa Ruiz) and falls in love. The trouble is, Carmen is a devoted Catholic. In order to win her heart, Stu has to become one as well. Initially pretending to be a believer – he even gets baptized in order to impress her – Stu becomes a true convert following a motorbike accident that puts him in a coma. He claims that while he was out cold he met the Virgin Mary, and on reawakening he commits his life to God and begins training to become a priest.

Sadly, his training and ambitions are cut short by his illness, which sees him pass away at the age of fifty. Stay for the end credits to meet the real Father Stu.

There were only six people at the screening I attended, and it didn't set the box office on fire, but this movie is definitely worth seeing. Rarely have I seen a film that so clearly and simply explains the Christian faith. It is a remarkable story that deserves to be told, and has been told well.

A great rockabilly soundtrack accompanies Stu on his journey, and I recommend this film wholeheartedly.

Journey to Bethlehem (2023)

Director: Adam Anders
Starring: Fiona Palomo, Milo Manheim, Lecrae, Antonio Banderas

So many versions of the Nativity story have been told on film that we simply don't have the space to list them all here. Everyone from William Wyler (director of *Ben-Hur*) to the creators of *Monty Python* have had a go at portraying it on screen. But there's never been a version quite like this.

Writer and director Adam Anders is no stranger to success. As a music producer and writer, he has sold more than 100 million records in recent years. Working alongside some of the world's biggest stars, he had a massive hit on his hands with TV series *Glee* (2009), and his music can be heard on the soundtrack of Disney's *High School Musical* (2006).

Anders makes his directorial debut in the holiday pop musical *Journey to Bethlehem*, starring Fiona Palomo (Mary), Milo Manheim (Joseph) and Antonio Banderas (King Herod). I had the privilege of interviewing Adam, and he told me this project had been seventeen years in the making. As a Christian, he wanted to be true to the biblical account of Jesus' birth, but at the same time he opted to use his imagination in bringing life to the story. In so doing, Anders shows the effect that the news of Mary's pregnancy would have had on her family, and particularly on her betrothed, Joseph.

The film offers an unusual take on the three wise men, who provide comic relief, and in addition we get to meet Herod's son, who is given the awful task of killing the baby boys in Bethlehem. All this action is accompanied by a succession of great new pop songs combined with traditional Christmas music. These songs range from the funny to the sad, from uplifting praise to down-to-earth realism about the situation as it unfolds.

I have a feeling that, for many of us, this film – and its soundtrack – will become part of our Christmas tradition in the future in the same way that *The Muppet Christmas Carol* or *Die Hard* have. It is a bright, lively movie with a reminder from the start that this is the greatest story ever told – even if Anders admits to taking a few liberties.

Jurassic World: Dominion (2020)

Director: Colin Trevorrow
Starring: Bryce Dallas Howard, Chris Pratt, Laura Dern

I was surprised that this movie had no preview screenings, no advance midnight showings and no triple bill with the previous two. It's normally a bad sign – a sign that the studio has a lack of confidence in the film. Indeed, most of the early press reviews were less than positive.

Having seen the film, I can see why. It basically offered more of the same, and while there are some good set pieces and even bigger dinosaurs, I just felt the whole thing fell a bit flat.

I have always enjoyed the *Jurassic* films – both *Park* and *World* – though for me it has been a law of diminishing returns. I confess that I have grown slightly less interested with each passing film.

If, as we are led to believe, this turns out to be the final movie of the series, it's probably about time. To be honest, the magic has somewhat evaporated. I saw *Jurassic Park* the day it opened, way back in 1993, and there was a time when we all sat in awe and wonder at the sight of 'real', living, breathing dinosaurs. We were thrilled at the sight of herds of them sweeping across the plains of Jurassic Park, and we gripped our seats in terror as the T-rex bore down on us. Let's be honest, we take such special effects for granted these days. We aren't surprised any more. We've lost that childhood sense of wonder that once gripped us.

Going in to see this one, I was hoping for something really new. But as I've already said, it was basically business as usual. The cast is fine, and it's nice to see the original stars back. Jeff Goldblum gets the best and funniest lines, and there's a nice tie-up to end the saga. The special effects are as you would expect, and it's good to hear echoes of John Williams's classic theme woven into Michael Giacchino's score.

I won't go into detail about the plot here, but expect a few good set pieces and quite a lot of exposition in the first half of the film (which really slowed things down for me). I would agree with *Empire* magazine's 3 out of 5 rating.

The Eyes of Tammy Faye (2021)

Director: Michael Showalter
Starring: Jessica Chastain, Andrew Garfield

Tammy Bakker (brilliantly played by Jessica Chastain) describes her face as her trademark at one point in this remarkable biopic about a remarkable couple. Indeed, she and her husband Jim Bakker (Andrew Garfield) did become two of the most recognisable, influential and powerful people in the US during the 1970s – even gaining the ear of world leaders. But this is a story about how the mighty fell… and fall they did.

When Jim and Tammy met at the North Central Bible College in Minneapolis in 1960, there can be little doubt that both were motivated to go out and tell the world about Jesus for good reasons. Both sincerely believed that God had big plans for them, and after their marriage in 1961 they began to pursue those dreams. They set up a travelling ministry and quickly became popular with church congregations through the charismatic preaching of Jim, and through Tammy's powerful singing voice and her use of puppets to attract family audiences. After meeting televangelist Pat Robertson, they quickly found a platform for their message, which grew and grew... and grew.

Eventually, they launched their own TV station, homes for the poor and even a Christian theme park. Their rise to international stardom was meteoric. But there was a serpent in the garden, and when temptation reared its ugly head, the couple gave in to it. Both had affairs, and Jim began cheating on the tax office before being outed as gay. Tammy's insistence that the Church should embrace the LGBTQ community did not go down well with the conservative evangelical majority. The result was that the ministry collapsed, the marriage ended in divorce and Jim spent eight years in prison.

This film tells that story, and tells it very well. Both Garfield and Chastain give remarkable performances, and while there is nothing particularly special about the direction, the film holds your attention throughout the two-hours-plus running time. It does this by appealing to our emotions throughout. We go from being excited about what these two could achieve to feeling disgusted by their actions, then to feeling a degree of sympathy and understanding for them. Ultimately, we recognise that their downfall was of their own making.

This film attracted a wide audience because of the two main stars, but it also caused people to think carefully about the motives of anyone who asks for money in exchange for ministry. It is incredibly entertaining and definitely worth your time. If there is power in words, then this film cautions us to be careful about who we listen to.

The Great Escaper (2023)

Director: Oliver Parker
Starring: Michael Caine, Glenda Jackson

During a recent tour of the Royal Albert Hall, I asked our tour guide how the poppies that fall during the annual Remembrance Day service are released. I was told that they are manually dropped through a small hole in the attic of the hall. Every one represents a life tragically lost. We know the names of many, and can visit their final resting places in cemeteries across Europe. Others will forever remain anonymous.

One name you may know well is that of Bernard Jordan. His name made national headlines back in the summer of 2014. Bernard (89), a Second World War veteran and D-Day survivor, was living with his wife Irene in a nursing home in Hove. Having unsuccessfully applied for tickets for the seventieth anniversary D-Day commemorations in France, he simply left the home early one morning, hopped on a train for Bournemouth and got on a ferry for France… and he made it! He even linked up with other veterans along the way. The issue was, he didn't tell anyone what he was doing or where he was going. As a result, his absence sparked a frantic search.

His and Irene's story was recently told in an excellent

new film called *The Great Escaper*. Michael Caine turns in a superb, funny and touching performance as Bernard, and proves that even at the age of ninety he's still one of Britain's greatest actors. Speaking of which, Glenda Jackson plays Irene, the only other person who had any idea about what was going on. Sadly, this would prove to be Glenda's last film role before her untimely death in June 2023. She's terrific in this film and plays the part with a real twinkle in her eye.

I absolutely loved *The Great Escaper*. It's superb. Everything about it is just right, and you really should see it. It also provides a helpful reminder, for any that needed it, of the debt of gratitude we owe to those who never came home – and to those who did.

We will remember them.

The Trouble With Jessica (2023)

Director: Matt Winn
Starring: Shirley Henderson, Alan Tudyk, Rufus Sewell

This movie is inspired by Hitchcock's 1955 film *The Trouble with Harry*, a black comedy in which the residents of a small hamlet try to decide what to do with an inconveniently placed dead body, Harry. This was the film that introduced Shirley MacLaine to the world.

Skip forward to 2023 and we have the same basic scenario, only this time the setting is a posh London home, where a dinner party is taking place. Successful London couple Sarah (Shirley Henderson) and Tom (Alan Tudyk) are in deep financial trouble. Things take a terrifying turn when, between courses, an uninvited dinner guest, Jessica (Indira Varma), decides to hang herself in the garden. With a prospective buyer for the house announcing he's about to come round and a nosy neighbour putting in an unwanted appearance, the question becomes what to do with the body. The resulting chaos is both hilarious and very dark. This is a wonderfully entertaining film with a top-notch British cast.

Oppenheimer/Barbie (2023)

Oppenheimer
Director: Christopher Nolan
Starring: Cillian Murphy, Florence Pugh, Robert Downey Jr.

Barbie
Director: Greta Gerwig
Starring: Margot Robbie, Ryan Gosling

So, here's a question for you: what do Bond, Spiderman, the man who invented the atom bomb and Barbie have in common? The answer is that they have all been described as 'saviours of cinema'. After the pandemic, cinemas had to fight hard to win audiences back. Their hopes were riding on the success or failure of several blockbusters that were meant to be real crowd-pleasers. By and large, films like *No Time to Die*, *Spider-Man: Across the Spider-Verse* (2023) and *Tenet* (2020) all did well at the box office and helped to bring the crowds back.

That said, not every major release is a success. For example, *Indiana Jones and the Dial of Destiny* was deemed a box office failure within two weeks of its release. *Mission: Impossible – Dead Reckoning Part One* (2023) did slightly better, but still wasn't a runaway success.

So it was that many a cinema manager had 21 July 2023 circled in their diaries. Would Christopher Nolan's latest epic, *Oppenheimer* – a biopic about the man who created the atomic bomb – and *Barbie* be the saviours that cinema chains had been praying for?

Oppenheimer: For me, it actually wasn't great. It was very, very good, but not great. You have to concentrate due to the non-linear storytelling, and I felt as if the last forty-five minutes or so dragged a bit. But the film also featured strong performances, script, score and effects.

Barbie: This film was a four out of ten, for me. (I initially gave it a seven, but have since rewatched, reconsidered and listened to others who didn't rate it. Always a good thing to do!) It's a bit all over the place, and given that its producers must have known young children would be taken to see it, it is not a film for youngsters at all. In fact, many of the jokes, apart from the opening scene, fall with a heavy thud and would go right over the heads of any twelve-year-olds watching. Ryan Gosling is very good as Ken and you have to say that Margot Robbie looks just as Barbie should look, but that's about it.

The Holdovers (2023)

Director: Alexander Payne
Starring: Paul Giamatti, Da'Vine Joy Randloph

I wrote the following at nearly midnight on 11 January 2024 from the Central London Press Screening. Now, it's not often that I say this, so brace yourselves… this film gets a ten out of ten from me and it's going to become part of my new Christmas tradition. It's such a shame *The Holdovers* didn't come out a few weeks earlier, as it would surely have been a Christmas hit.

With undertones of *Dead Poets Society* (1989) and *The Breakfast Club* (1985), and shot in a style that reminded me of *The Graduate* (1967 – Simon and Garfunkel-like songs accompany quite a few scenes, with a score to match), this story of a disliked history teacher, a dysfunctional teenager and a bereaved school cook having to spend Christmas together at their boarding school is quite simply cinematic gold.

David Hemingson's script is as sharp as a pin and Alexander Payne directs with an incredible eye for detail. We are back in 1970, and the way the film is shot never left me in any doubt of that. The film smashes the 'six-laugh test', yet is also deeply moving and thought-provoking.

The performances are all top-notch. All three leads make the roles their own. The Golden Globes got it right (Paul Giamatti won Best Actor – Motion Picture Musical or Comedy and Da'Vine Joy Randolph won Best Supporting Actress), and I'm confident more awards are to come. If there's any justice, there will be.

I haven't felt this way about any film since I saw *Typist Artist Pirate King*. It's an absolute must-see and already a candidate for my top ten of 2024 list. I know, I know, but boy are films this year going to have to be good to match this.

Cabrini (2023)

Director: Alejandro Gómez Monteverde
Starring: Christiana Dell'Anna, David Morse

This powerful and compelling true story is so beautifully shot that it draws you in from the very first frame and refuses to let you go. Brought to us by Angel Studios (also responsible for *The Chosen* (2017) and *Sound of Freedom* (2023), among other great films) in conjunction with World Mission, it's easy to see why the presale figures exceeded $1 million. It certainly deserved to be a massive worldwide hit.

Set in 1889 (the attention to period detail is astonishing), *Cabrini* tells the true story of a very determined woman. Cristiana Dell'Anna plays Francis Cabrini, a real-life Italian immigrant who arrives in New York determined to provide an orphanage and homes for the poor and downcast of the city. Despite having the approval of the pope for her mission, she initially meets with hostility, bigotry, racism and violence. Nevertheless, she remains determined to build a better world, right in the heart of the growing metropolis.

The strength of Cabrini's faith is remarkable in the face

of overwhelming odds, and Dell'Anna is terrific in the title role. She encapsulates a kind, compassionate, caring woman who is determined to achieve her goal at all costs. This should have been an awards-nominated performance.

The film has some wonderful set pieces and scenes that will move, shock and horrify. The film serves as a vivid reminder that, although it is set back in the 1800s, the needs of the destitute are just as real today. Skilfully directed – there's almost a photo-realistic quality to some scenes – the film also has a beautiful score.

The story, which I didn't previously know, is one that is certainly worth telling, and it's been brought to life in a riveting way. I have no hesitation in thoroughly recommending this wonderful, thought-provoking and compelling film.

Appendix: Evangelistic film nights at your church

I was recently invited to a church in Essex that was celebrating its one hundredth anniversary. As part of the outreach, the congregation decided to turn their church into a cinema for the day. Serving hotdogs and popcorn, they erected a big screen and showed the film *Risen* (see below). It worked! A number of people from the village came – including one lady who had lived there all her life but had never been inside the building.

Evangelistic film nights are a proven way of reaching out and getting people into our churches to hear the good news of Jesus. Many films lend themselves to the gospel, and many can be used to open up discussions. On a dark winter's night, inviting people in to see a film is a fantastic way of sharing the gospel.

First, a word about showing movies in churches.

Location: How many people can you accommodate? How many are you hoping to reach? If you are simply planning to deliver a talk after a film, the size of the venue doesn't really matter, but if you're planning to have a group discussion, a smaller, more comfortable, venue where people can sit around in a group is better.

Projection: Use the best equipment and biggest screen available.

Refreshments: Provide popcorn and other snacks, and allow for comfort breaks.

Discussion: As always when talking to people who are not Christians, nothing is out of bounds; nothing is too shocking; no question is too easy or too embarrassing.

Summary sheets: Why not provide a fact sheet about the film being discussed with a list of questions it raises? These can be handed out before the film, so that group members can be thinking about them as they watch.

A question to bear in mind while we watch movies together: can films make us better people?

In Darren Aronofsky's 2014 film *Noah*, Ray Winstone plays a hard, tough rebel, Tubal-cain, who is determined to get on board the ark at any cost once the rain starts to fall. At one point he makes a rallying cry, declaring that 'men united' are unbeatable. However, at the screening I attended, one audience member shouted out, 'No they're not – Chelsea are!' It was so funny I forgave the interruption.

But this raises an interesting question: how invincible are our heroes – particularly in the movies? From the response of many to the final scene of *No Time to Die*, it would appear that we not only expect our heroes to be good-looking, charming and street smart – but above all else, we expect them to be invincible.

Killing off Bond was a bold move by the producers, and one that reminds us all of our mortality. For my part, I think that is to be commended. We all need to face the fact that we will pass on one day, which should spur us on to make the most of each day. As a Christian – a disciple of Jesus Christ – I believe that because Jesus died on the cross to pay the price for my wrongdoings, and because he rose again, I will find myself in heaven when death comes. So the question is less about when we will die and more about how we're going to spend the time between now and then.

Of course, most movie heroes do live to fight another day. At last count, Detective McClane has died hard five times. Despite rumours to the contrary, Jason Bourne has survived through four films and Wonder Woman has defied death on countless occasions.

However, the reality is that few of us will end up engaging in any sort of superhuman lifestyle. The best most of us can hope for is a satisfying job, enough money to pay the mortgage, with maybe a bit to spare, a nice holiday now and then, and a lovely, loyal family. There's nothing wrong with any of those things, of course. In fact, given the world we live in, that sounds like a pretty good way to spend our three score and ten years. But can the movies help us become better at... well... being human?

Movie suggestions
Here are a few suggestions of movies that might help us find ways to transform into the kind of people we aspire to be, regardless of the hand life has dealt us. I've picked five that seem pertinent, but I'm sure you'll be able to think of many, many more. Some may seem like odd choices, but bear with me.

1. *The Truman Show* (1998)
The underlying messages of this film are as follows: life can be confusing, and we may never achieve all our ambitions, but don't give up on them. Keep going, keep trying. Be nice to everyone and they will be nice to you. And as for the boy or girl of your dreams – do everything it takes to be with him/her.

As a Christian, I believe God is up there watching over me and that everything will be OK. (I always found it interesting that the creator and director of The Truman Show – the show within the movie – is called *Christ*of.) This film encourages us to chase our dreams. Even if they don't come true, at least we will have the satisfaction of knowing that we tried.

Discussion questions
1. What does the film have to say about society? Do you feel you have the freedom you are entitled to?
2. How do you feel about the concept of God watching over us – seeing everything we do? Does that make you

feel uncomfortable or does it give you a sense of security?
3. What makes life worth living? What should our priorities be? Is it possible to be truly happy in this world?
4. Do you believe in evolution or creation – or a mix of both? In light of this, are we responsible for our own actions or will we answer to a higher authority one day?
5. Why do you think the writers of the film named the creator of The Truman Show *Christ*of?

2. *Death Becomes Her* (1992)

A strange choice maybe, but check it out. Having just played all-action hero John McClane in box office smash *Die Hard*, Bruce Willis went on to play the weak, subservient and rather pathetic Ernest Menville in this science-fiction comedy. The film's lessons are: don't be consumed by the way you look; be careful who you fall in love with; and don't allow yourself to be dominated – even by a formidable pair like Meryl Streep and Goldie Hawn.

Discussion questions

1. What makes a man a man and a woman a woman? How would you define 'real' manhood/womanhood?
2. Can we control who we fall in love with? In a world of quick divorce and broken relationships, what makes for stable relationships and strong marriages?
3. How far would you go for the person you love?
4. What does standing up for ourselves look like?
5. What do you think of Jesus? In what ways did he show himself to be a 'real man'?
6. Is it weak to say, 'I love Jesus'? Is he worth following?

3. *Schindler's List* (1993)
There comes a time when every one of us must examine ourselves to ensure that we are doing the right thing and can live with our conscience, no matter what the personal cost may be. The theme of this film is: give yourself and your life for the sake of others, and you will discover what life is all about. Sacrifice is worth it in the end.

Discussion questions
1. If you were in Schindler's position, what would you do? Would you have had the courage to do what he did?
2. What is the biggest sacrifice you have ever had to make? What did it cost and how did it make you feel?
3. What are your priorities in life? Who or what are the most important things in your life right now? What would you do to protect or save them?
4. At the end of the film, Schindler says he wishes he could have saved just one more person. How did the film make you feel?
5. The Bible describes God sacrificing his own Son for the sake of humanity. How does this make you feel? What is your view of the core message of Christianity?

4. The *Indiana Jones* films (1981-present)
The underlying themes throughout the Indy films are: set yourself goals and go for them. Learn to deal with the past, but take the time to correct the mistakes you have made. Fortune and glory aren't worth it if they require you to sell your soul. Prove to others that you are trustworthy, and they will follow you – even into the Well of Souls or Temple of Doom.

Discussion questions
1. An awful lot of us dream about being like Indiana Jones or Lara Croft. What does that kind of lifestyle offer, and do you think it would be truly satisfising?
2. If you could go on an amazing adventure, what would it be?
3. What are your aims and goals in real life, and how can you fulfil them?
4. Do you think faith can help you lead a fulfilled life? What did Jesus mean when he said that he came so that we could have life, and have it to the full?
5. What makes life worth living?

5. *Risen* (2016)
My favourite 'Christian movie' of all time. Joseph Fiennes plays a battle-hardened Roman soldier, Clavius, who is present at the crucifixion and burial of Christ. A few days later, as rumours that this Jesus has come back to life begin to spread, he is tasked with producing the body of Jesus to dispel the rumours.

It's a terrific film because, as he pursues Jesus's disciples – who he is convinced have stolen the body – Clavius encounters the risen Christ and becomes a follower himself. It's a beautiful, dramatic film that reminds us that following Jesus is the best – and only – way to make the most of life.

Discussion questions
1. Do you believe in the resurrection of Jesus? If not, why not?
2. (Group leaders could present some evidence of the

resurrection before asking the following question.) Is it at all possible that Jesus may actually have risen from the dead?

3. What difference would it make to you if the resurrection was proved to be true?

4. Did the film offer a convincing portrayal of what may have happened after Jesus died?

5. What questions do you have about the Christian faith?

So… are we invincible? No, as the last Bond film reminds us. Can life be fulfilling, satisfying and worth living? Yes, but only when lived with God at the centre, as Clavius discovered. In the end, the way we choose to live is up to us. Choose wisely!

Acknowledgements

I am enormously grateful to so many people for their help, encouragement, wisdom and advice while I was writing this book. This is my first attempt, and while combining two of my greatest passions, movies and my faith, has been fun and exciting, it has also been a labour of love.

So, without further ado…

Massive thanks to Mum, for all your help and support. To my brother Tim and sister-in-law Maz, for keeping my feet on the ground. Thank you to my good friend Iain Shaddick for encouraging me to give it a go, and sitting with me through many a disappointing – and sometimes good – Bristol City game (another passion of mine). Even if you did fall asleep during *Oppenheimer*! Also, to my friends Andrea and Mark for spurring me on. Thank you to Mark Kermode for teaching me so much about being a film critic. I love your style, sir.

A very special and massive thank you to my very good friends Steve and Bekah Legg. It was Steve who trusted me to write film reviews for *Sorted*, and it's been thrilling to see a quote from the magazine on a dozen or so movie posters. It's also been a privilege to share a little in Steve's ongoing battle with cancer and to be with him at various events promoting *Sorted*. Love you guys.

This book would not be in your hands without the help, skill and advice of two wonderful ladies: my editor, Joy Tibbs, and my designer, Esther Kotecha. Thank you both so much. You have been amazing. Also, many thanks to Nathan from Pure247radio.org for your willingness to read the book and make some helpful comments.

Finally, thank you to my wonderful Lord and Saviour, who has met my every need over the years and given me the privilege of sharing in what is, without a doubt, **the greatest story ever told**.

THE MOVIE
Reviewer

COMING TO A CHURCH NEAR YOU NOW!

Witness the Insight.

Embrace the Expertise.

Don't miss the chance to experience thought-provoking discussions, deep dives into your favourite films, and a fresh perspective on faith and the art of cinema.

Join Us for an Unforgettable Journey Through Film!

For showtimes and more information, book now:

a.godfrey5862@gmail.com

Be there. Be inspired.

★★★★★
Sorted Magazine

★★★★★
Hope FM

★★★★★
Stuart Pascall - Moorlands

NEVER MISS A COPY
WHEN YOU
SUBSCRIBE TO SORTED

Come on.
Do it now.
Get Sorted.

Go online at **sortedmag.com** or scan the QR code

"How long have I got, Doc? Five days? Five weeks? Five months? Five years?" "More like months," the oncologist replied.

When he heard this devasting news, Steve and his wife Bekah made a bold decision - they would get busy living and get busy laughing. Yes, there were tears that day and in those that followed, but Steve is a funnyman and a man of faith. He was never going to give cancer the last laugh.

'I couldn't put it down – laughing, brushing away a tear and going on a journey with Steve, the funnyman as he faced the no-joke reality of the diagnosis of a terminal illness. But this is not just Steve's story; he draws lessons that can change not only the way we view our death – but also our life.'

Rob Parsons OBE, author of *The Heart of Success*

Available at
amazon

or scan below

scm

MEN'S HEALTH MATTERS PODCAST
With
Steve Legg
& Dr Ken
LISTEN TO THIS PODCAST ON:
music
deezer

Printed in Great Britain
by Amazon